Needlework Dragons and Other Mythical Creatures

Carol Gault

Needlework Dragons
AND OTHER
Mythical Creatures

PRENTICE HALL PRESS · NEW YORK

For Nicholas, who still believes in mythical beasts;
for Gordon, who cleans up after them;
and for Shirley, who taught me how to create them.

Published in 1987 by Prentice Hall Press
A Division of Simon & Schuster, Inc.
Gulf + Western Building
One Gulf + Western Plaza
New York, NY 10023

Originally published in hardcover by Van Nostrand Reinhold
Company, Inc.

PRENTICE HALL PRESS is a trademark
of Simon & Schuster, Inc.

Library of Congress Cataloging-in-Publication Data

Gault, Carol.
Needlework dragons and other mythical creatures.
Bibliography: p.
Includes index.
1. Needlework—Patterns.   2. Design, Decorative—
Animal forms.   I. Title.
TT753.G381983746.44'04182-24853
ISBN 0-671-60994-7
ISBN 0-13-611336-2 (pbk.)

Designed by Karolina Harris

Manufactured in the United States of America

10 9 8 7 6 5 4 3 2 1

Contents

Introduction

1 Materials   **9**

2 Techniques   **13**

3 Finishing Hints   **18**

4 Chinatown Dragon Needlepoint Pillow   **24**

5 Dragon in the Sea Needlepoint Wall Hanging   **30**

6 Unicorn and Griffin Needlepoint Pillows   **42**

7 Enchanted Land Needlepoint Pillow and Phoenix Needlepoint Wall Hanging   **49**

8 Taiyuin Needlepoint Pillow   **60**

9 Cherry Blossom Flower Child Cross-Stitch Stationery Portfolio   **64**

10 California Poppy Flower Child Cross-Stitch Framed Picture   **69**

11 Rose Baby Cross-Stitch Book Cover   **72**

12 Dragon Blackwork Framed Picture   **75**

13 Mythical Character Cross-Stitch Alphabet Projects   **78**

14 Sea Serpent and Pegasus Cross-Stitch Fabric Boxes   **100**

15 Heracles and Achelous Cross-Stitch Pillow   **106**

16 Mythical Beast Appliqué Quilt   **110**

17 Pegasus Needlepoint Clutch Purse   **134**

18 Phoenix Blackwork Mounted Picture   **137**

19 Green Dragon Needlepoint Pillow   **140**

Bibliography   **142**

Index   **143**

Acknowledgments

No enterprise this large can be done without the help of many people. My family and my friends encouraged me, allowed me to pick their brains for information, and spent numerous hours—with needles in hand—stitching, stitching their fingers to the bone.

I want to thank my stitchers—Karen Benight, Leslie Armistead, Kate Johnson, Elizabeth Lucasi, Jennifer Robinson, Denise Charlesworth, Joann Young, Colleen Fairbairn, Wendy Gault, and Pam Trask—for all the holes they poked in their fingers. I want to thank Howard Schulman for his patience in finding just the right light for photographing needlework. Thank you, Jenny Stone, for typing. Special thanks to Shirley Carlton for all the design lessons; to Carol Sherley for needlepoint classes; to Carol Algie for the blackwork class; and to Susan Gies for teaching me how to put a book together.

Most important, I want to thank Gordon, my resident biochemist, who tolerates bits of yarn, needles, quilting and needlepoint frames, project bags, and drafting supplies all over the house without too much complaint, and Nicholas, my resident critic, who knows exactly what he likes.

Introduction

My favorite stories, as a child, were fairy tales and ancient myths. Even as an adult, I prefer stories that have fantastic or magical creatures. After having worked in a local needlecraft store for a few years, I was asked by the San Francisco Embroiderer's Guild to design a dragon for the rug commemorating San Francisco's bicentennial. I felt challenged by a project that appealed to my love of fantastic beasts. I had never designed needlepoint before; but with a little help from my friends, I found pictures and colors to get started, and I completed my interpretation of the *Chinatown Dragon.* Since that time, I have kept my eyes open for designs of fantasy to interpret with my needle and thread.

My fingers have been busy doing needlework since my mother taught me to knit and my grandmother taught me to embroider. Everywhere I go I pick up new techniques and learn new skills by watching and listening to other needleworkers. Over the years I've perfected my skills in needlework and learned a tremendous amount about design. To share my delight with needlework and fantasy, I have created these mythical creature projects for other people to stitch.

I have never been happy doing just one kind of needlework. I find that a wide variety of projects helps keep me inspired and creative all the time. This book provides a wide choice of techniques and designs to inspire anyone who likes mythical beasts. There are needlepoint pillows and wall hangings, cross-stitch boxes, an appliqué bedspread and a blackwork dragon, to mention but a few projects. Many of the designs can be used for more than one technique. The quilt designs can be used for needlepoint or blackwork; the needlepoint designs can be used for counted cross-stitch as well. There are many different ways you can use these designs, once you have finished stitching them. Framed pictures and pillows are just two examples; but there are book covers, portfolios, and purses to be made as well.

For those people who are trying some of the techniques for the first time or simply need review, there are helpful hints and stitch diagrams throughout the book. I recommend you read these hints before beginning a project to prevent confusion. Even if you don't need a refresher course, you might pick up a new hint. For more instruction consult the bibliography; here you will find books that contain more detailed information on techniques.

It is my fondest hope that the designs in this book will inspire the beginner and challenge the expert, and I trust the variety of projects will give devoted stitchers some new ideas for their needlework. Mythical beasts have been a part of our history and culture. When we are children they are given reality in our stories. Everyone needs their own personal dragon living on their wall, or a Pegasus flying on their purse, or a unicorn sitting in their favorite chair.

Have a marvelous time creating a myth in thread.

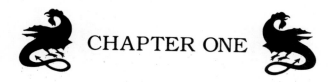

CHAPTER ONE

Materials

I have been doing some kind of needlecraft most of my life, and my biggest disappointments were the direct result of my having used poor quality materials. If you are going to spend your precious time making a needlework project, use the best quality materials you can find. For each project in this book, there is a list of materials you will need to complete the design. I have given brand names to give you a starting place, but there are many other brands of quality that can be substituted. The information that follows is a brief description of the materials you'll need.

THREADS

Generally, for most types of thread, lengths should be approximately 18 inches (46cm) to avoid knots and tangles. For a smoother texture and better coverage, separate the individual plies of the stranded threads and recombine the appropriate number of plies, following the directions for the project.

Persian yarn is a versatile 3 ply wool that comes in a wide variety of colors. Persian yarn can be used in different sizes of canvas by separating the plies until you have the thickness required. It is generally used for needlepoint, but can be used for surface embroidery as well.

Embroidery floss is a 6 ply cotton thread. It works well for embroidery, needlepoint, and cross-stitch, and there are many available colors from which to choose. It separates into individual plies, which makes it versatile for lots of different projects. Although none of the projects calls for silk floss, it can be substituted for cotton when you

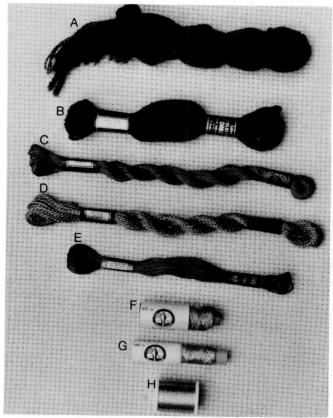

Figure 1-1. *A.* Persian Yarn *B.* Tapestry Yarn *C.* Perle Cotton (size 5) *D.* Perle Cotton (size 3) *E.* Embroidery Floss *F.* Cord Metallic *G.* Blending Filament *H.* Metallic Thread.

would like a more elegant alternative. Silk is more expensive and difficult to handle but it is longer lasting and luxurious.

Tapestry yarn is a wool thread that does *not* separate into plies, but is used as a complete strand for needlepoint, crewel embroidery, and cross-stitch.

Perle cotton is a cotton thread that is used as a complete strand. It comes in different sizes for different needlepoint canvas sizes and embroidery thicknesses.

Metallic threads come in a wide variety of thicknesses and colors. They are used as single strands or in conjunction with other threads for needlepoint and surface embroidery. Cut metallic thread lengths a bit shorter than cottons and wools because they fray and shred easily. If you dip the thread end in some clear nail polish, let it dry, and thread your needle with the nail polish end, it will help alleviate this problem.

FABRICS

All the projects in this book involve some kind of fabric. Cross-stitch decorates fabric, and the fabric becomes part of the design. Needlepoint creates a new fabric when all the mesh is filled in with stitches. Appliqué creates a design out of fabric.

Needlepoint canvas is a cotton mesh available in sizes that are counted in threads per inch; for example, #14 has 14 threads per inch. If you want to change the size of a design in the book you can do so by changing the canvas size accordingly. To make it larger, use a canvas with fewer threads per inch. To make it smaller, use a canvas with more threads per inch.

Even-weave fabrics, used for counted thread embroidery, are available in all different fibers and colors. They are sized by how many stitches can be made per inch. For example, #14 Aida cloth has 14 squares per inch. As with needlepoint canvas (see above), you can change the size of a design by using a different size fabric. Aida cloth (pronounced like the opera) is a cotton fabric that is woven in obvious squares. Each square is used for one cross-stitch. Fiddler's cloth is a cotton-linen-polyester blend that is woven like Aida cloth. It is a natural colored (not dyed or bleached) fabric. Hardanger is a cotton plain-weave fabric. The threads must be counted for cross-stitch or blackwork—there are no obvious squares. You can make as many as 22 stitches per inch, or you can double the size by counting 2 threads per stitch, resulting in 11 stitches per inch. In addition to the cotton even-weaves, there are linen, wool, and polyester even-

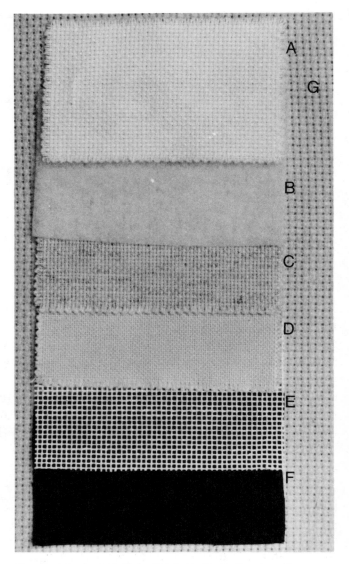

Figure 1-2. *A.* #14 Aida Cloth *B.* Quilt Batting *C.* Fiddler's Cloth *D.* Hardanger *E.* Needlepoint Canvas *F.* Broadcloth *G.* #7 Wool Java (background).

weave fabrics that are similar in weave to the cotton fabrics described.

Pure cotton or cotton/polyester broadcloth is used for the quilting and appliqué projects. These lightweight fabrics are available at most yard goods stores in a wide variety of colors and prints. They are easy to work with, and they wear well.

Quilt batting is a nonwoven filler for quilted projects. It comes in several different thicknesses and is usually made of cotton, a cotton/polyester blend, or polyester. If it has a high cotton content, more quilting needs to be done to hold the batting together. Thin batting is easier to quilt than the thicker varieties.

NEEDLES

Needles are available with different kinds of eyes and points. The type you use will depend on the thread and fabric called for in the project.

Tapestry needles have a dull point and a large eye. They are used for needlepoint, counted cross-stitch, and blackwork.

Embroidery needles have a sharp point and a large eye. They are used for embroidery stitches that require piercing the fabric.

Quilting needles are short with a sharp point and a small eye.

Sharps are the standard sewing needle with a sharp point. They are used for appliqué and hand sewing.

Upholstery needles have a sharp point and are curved. They are used to finish different projects that are difficult to sew with a straight needle.

MISCELLANEOUS SUPPLIES

Every good needleworker has a workbox of miscellaneous supplies she can easily lay her hands on.

Marking pens for needlepoint canvas must be waterproof so they won't run when the canvas is blocked. They are used to transfer the pattern onto the canvas or to make guide lines. I prefer the gray Nepo marker because it doesn't show through under light colors.

Quilting pencils are available in white and blue for drawing guide lines and tracing pattern shapes onto fabric. If they are used lightly and not ironed in, they wash out of the fabric with soapy water.

Embroidery transfer pens and pencils will transfer an embroidery pattern onto fabric by rubbing or ironing. Make sure they will wash out after the stitching is completed by testing a sample first.

Embroidery hoops will hold your cross-stitch,

Figure 1-3. *A.* Tapestry Needles *B.* Embroidery Needles *C.* Quilting Needles *D.* Upholstery Needles.

Figure 1-4. *A.* Magnetic Board *B.* Nepo Markers *C.* Transfer Pen *D.* Quilting Pencil *E.* Braided Persian *F.* Floss Holders *G.* Needlepoint Frame *H.* Embroidery Hoop *I.* Sewing Shears *J.* Thimble *K.* Needle Threader *L.* Embroidery Scissors *M.* Quilting Templates.

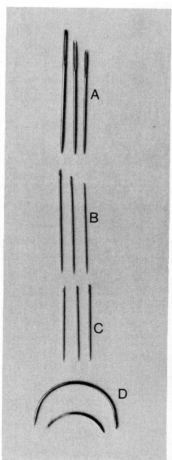

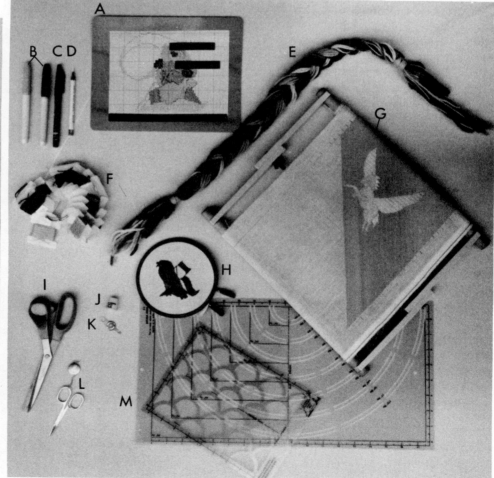

appliqué fabric, or embroidery taut. This prevents the stitches from puckering when they are pulled through the fabric. Hoops come in a wide variety of sizes—for small embroidery projects up to large quilting projects.

Needlepoint frames hold needlepoint canvas straight so that little blocking will be needed upon completion of the project.

Quilting frames make quilting a large quilt easier. They help hold the layers together evenly so puckers are not as likely to occur.

Shears should be sharp for cutting fabric. A pair of small, pointed embroidery scissors is very useful for clipping unwanted threads close to the project so tails are not hanging in the back.

Thimbles are not always necessary when doing needlework. But they do help you to poke needles through uncooperative fabric, and they protect your fingers from holes caused by pushing a needle too much.

Needle threaders are available to help get uncooperative thread through the small eyes on needles.

Magnetic line keepers are available to mark your place on a chart as you work on needlepoint or cross-stitch. They also hold your place when you put your work down and return to it later.

Tracing paper is available at most art-supply stores. In the projects in this book, it is used to trace and enlarge patterns. For appliqué patterns, it is better to trace patterns onto fabric from tracing paper, rather than drawing paper, because light passes through tracing paper more easily.

Quilt templates can be purchased in standard patterns or can be made out of cardboard. They are used to draw the quilting lines on the fabric when the quilt top is completed.

Floss holders and yarn pallets are available to keep your threads orderly, instead of in a jumbled mass at the bottom of your bag. To keep track of color symbols, mark your floss and yarn organizers with labels showing the appropriate symbol for your yarn. Cards and curtain rings can also be used to organize yarn for a project. Another nice way of organizing Persian yarn is to braid all the colors loosely together, holding each end with a rubber band. Strands can be pulled out individually and the others are held neatly until they are needed.

NEEDLEWORK SUPPLIES

For mail-order needlework supplies write to:

Gault Designs
P.O. Box 60386
Palo Alto, CA 94306

Write to the following suppliers for the location of stores in your area that carry their products:

Johnson Creative Arts
(for Paternayan Persian yarn)
West Townsend, MA 01474

Chatalbash Rug Co., Inc.
(for Paternayan yarn, 1/2 lb. minimum)
245 Fifth Avenue
New York, NY 10016

DMC Corporation
(for DMC embroidery floss and Perle cotton)
107 Trumbull Street
Elizabeth, NJ 07206

Charles Craft
(for Aida cloth, Hardanger, canvas)
PO Box 1169
Lavrinbury, NC 28352

Joan Toggitt
(for Aida cloth, Hardanger, canvas)
246 Fifth Avenue
New York, NY 10001

Wichelt Imports, Inc.
(for Aida cloth, Hardanger, canvas)
RR#1
Stoddard, WI 54658

Pearl Art & Craft Suppliers
(for canvas)
2411 Hempstead Turnpike
East Meadow, NY 11554

Handwork Tapestries Inc.
(for wholesale canvas, 10 yd. minimum)
144 B Allen Boulevard
Farmingdale, NY 11735

Kreinik Mfg. Co.
(for Balger blending filament)
1351 Market Street
Parkersberg, WV 26101

Quilt Crafts
(for quilting frames; mail-order)
PO Box 1114
Corona, CA 91720

Sudberry House
(for wooden objects on which to mount)
Box 895
Old Lyme, CT 06371

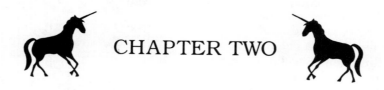

CHAPTER TWO

Techniques

This book is not intended to teach the basics of needlepoint, cross-stitch, embroidery, or quilting. There are so many readily available books with basic information that I couldn't possibly imitate them and have room for designs also. If you need more information, see the Bibliography for the books on techniques. What this section intends to do is provide helpful hints on the techniques used in the designs. Read the hints before starting projects and study the "how-to" diagrams for a quick review.

NEEDLEPOINT HINTS

The following hints should help you achieve quality needlepoint work.

To prevent canvas from unraveling, tape the edges of your canvas with masking tape.

The dimensions given in the materials include a 2-inch (5cm) margin around the design of unworked canvas. This is for blocking after the design is stitched. If you plan to change the canvas size, be sure to include this margin in your calculations.

Work your design with the selvage (the densely-woven edge that doesn't unravel) of the canvas on the right or left, rather than at the top or bottom of the design.

Use a waterproof marker to mark canvas (see *Materials*). Gray markers are best under light colors; black markers tend to show through under light colors.

Yarn has a smooth direction and a rough direction. Run your fingers along a strand and find the smooth direction. Thread the needle so that the smooth direction pulls through the canvas.

Do *not* knot the yarn. All ends should be tucked under the backs of 4 to 5 stitches or under previous work.

Try to keep the back of your work neat. Cut all the tails so that the colors won't fuzz into other colors.

A needlepoint frame is not necessary, but it will hold the design straighter and keep it cleaner. Once you get used to using it, your needlepoint work will go faster.

When finished, hold your work up to a strong light to locate any missed stitches.

Most of the needlepoint designs in this book were worked in one of the tent stitches. Continental and basketweave are tent stitches that look the same on the front but are worked differently. Basketweave does not pull the canvas out of shape as much as the continental does, so use basketweave to fill in large areas of color. A combination of continental and basketweave stitches works very well for outlines.

Left-handed needleworkers do the mirror image of the directions shown. If right-handed stitchers start at the bottom of a stitch, left-handed stitchers start at the top of the stitch. If right-handed stitchers start at the right side of the canvas, left-handed people start at the left. See the Bibliography for books just for left-handed needlework.

The basketweave stitch should be worked as continuously as possible with no breaks except for color changes.

For basketweave stitch always alternate "up" and "down" rows. Two rows worked in the same direction consecutively will leave a ridge.

To keep track of the direction your basketweave stitching should be going, always work downward rows over the intersections that have the vertical canvas threads on top (see D in Figure 2-1) and work the upward rows over intersections that have the horizontal thread on top (see E in Figure 2-1).

Tuck threads horizontally or vertically—*not* diagonally—to avoid ridges.

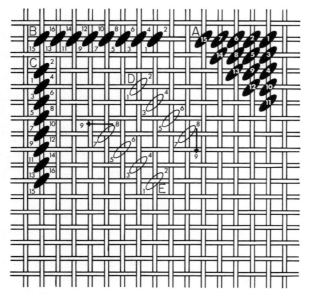

Figure 2-1. Tent Stitches. *A.* Stitch sequence of basketweave stitch *B.* Needle sequence of horizontal continental stitch *C.* Needle sequence of vertical continental stitch *D.* Needle sequence of downward row of basketweave stitch; notice vertical canvas thread *E.* Needle sequence of upward row of basketweave stitch; notice horizontal canvas thread.

CROSS-STITCH HINTS

Go over these hints for a basic cross-stitch review.

To prevent the fabric from unraveling, zigzag the edges on a sewing machine.

Use *no* knots. Tuck the ends under the backs of 4 to 5 stitches or under previous work.

For a smooth look, the top diagonal of the **X** should always be going in the same direction.

If you prefer, each **X** can be worked individually. Or you can work one row of diagonals, then work the top diagonal back across the row.

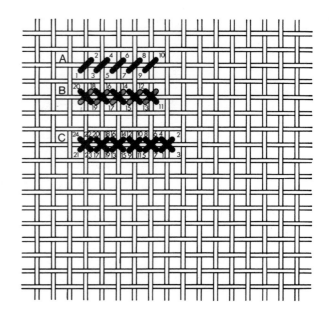

Figure 2-2. Cross-Stitch. *A.* Needle sequence of first row of diagonals *B.* Needle sequence of return row of diagonals *C.* Needle sequence for cross-stitches stitched individually.

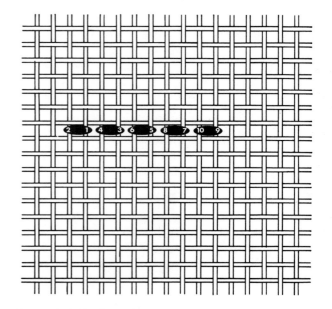

Figure 2-3. Backstitch.

The backstitch is worked on top of cross-stitching to highlight or emphasize certain parts of the design. When the pattern calls for backstitching, do this work after the whole design is cross-stitched. Backstitching is indicated by dark lines on the graph.

Hoops are not necessary for cross-stitch, but are sometimes helpful.

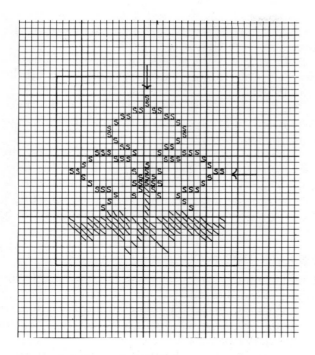

Figure 2-4. Cross-Stitch chart.

Code	Color
⌷ss	light green
⌷⁄⁄	dark green

FOLLOWING GRAPHS FOR NEEDLEPOINT OR CROSS-STITCH

Following graphs is easy to do if you follow a few simple guidelines.

Each square equals 1 stitch.

Baste fabric or mark canvas through the vertical and horizontal centers to provide a good reference line.

Start at the center of a design to ensure that the design will be properly centered on the canvas or fabric. It's not necessary, however, if you have lots of extra canvas or fabric—or if you're a good counter.

Do not try to do all of one color at one time, jumping from one design area to another. The easiest way to miscount is to skip across unworked canvas or fabric. Fill in each of the colors out from your starting place as you come to it in the graph. This will make it easier to find counting errors and prevent having to rip out large areas because a stitch or two was misplaced.

To keep track of colors and symbols, put the yarns through a card or ring with appropriate symbols marked next to the yarn.

QUILTING HINTS

The many good quilting books are invaluable aids, but the following tips should be helpful.

Use a template or work freehand to mark the quilting pattern lightly on the quilt top with a quilting pencil.

Sandwich the batting between the quilt top and the quilt bottom.

Test pencil, chalk, or marking pen on a scrap of fabric to make sure it washes out easily.

It is easier to baste the quilt top, batting, and quilt bottom together if everything is laid out flat on the floor or a large table.

Baste all three layers together starting at the center and sewing out to the edges.

Place quilt on a quilting frame or in a hoop to keep layers flat and to prevent puckering. To make quilting easier the quilt should be somewhat slack in the frame, not pulled taut like embroidery in a hoop.

Use a small, even running stitch along quilt pattern lines.

Hide the starting and ending knots in the batting layer by giving a sharp tug to pull the knot through the quilt top.

Start the quilting in the center of the design and quilt out toward the edges.

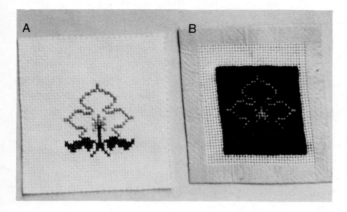

Figure 2-5. Examples showing completed stitching of the graph shown. *A.* Cross-stitch *B.* Needlepoint.

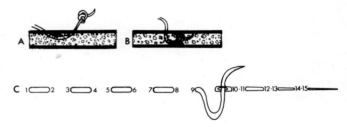

Figure 2-6. Quilting Techniques. *A and B.* Hiding the knot in the quilt batting at the beginning and end of a thread *C.* Quilt running stitch.

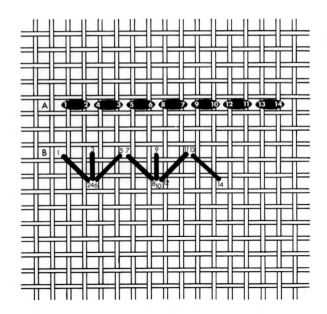

Figure 2-7. *A.* Back-forward stitch *B.* Stitch sequence of one geometric pattern.

BLACKWORK HINTS

Basically, any good embroidery advice will apply here also.

Use either backstitch or back-forward stitch to do geometric patterns.

A waste knot put several inches away from the design on the front of the fabric anchors the thread at the start of each new row. These knots are cut off when the work is complete, and the ends are wrapped around the back of the outline stitching.

The length of thread should be enough to com-

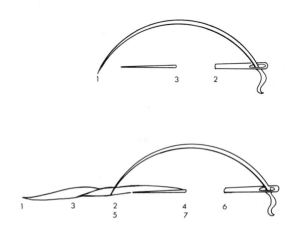

Figure 2-8. Stem stitch.

plete the row across the design. Always end the thread at an outline.

When a complete geometric pattern will not fit in an area, use a portion of that pattern to fill the available space.

Start the pattern at the widest part of the space to be filled. Fill in the rest of the space building out from the first row.

Take the smallest stitches possible across the back of the fabric. Long stitches across the back cause shadow effects on the front of the fabric.

The outline stitch can be started by splitting a small running stitch with a second running stitch.

ENLARGING A DESIGN

There are many different ways to enlarge a design to any size you need.

An opaque projector is the simplest method. A photostat machine will make a transparency of the design to use on an overhead projector. A slide of a design projected on the wall also works. In each case, the design is projected onto a piece of paper on the wall and traced onto that paper. The problem with these methods is lack of access to this equipment.

The alternative is to use a grid. Each design in this book that needs to be enlarged can be marked with a grid. By drawing a grid with larger squares and filling in each square with the design lines of the respective squares in the original, an enlarged version results. People who do not draw well are able to master this task if they work one square at a time. This method takes only time, paper, ruler, and pencil.

TRANSFERRING PATTERNS

Whether the design has to be enlarged or not, some designs will have to be transferred onto your fabric or canvas.

Needlepoint canvas is very easy to trace onto because of all the holes. Use a black marker to make a very dark outline on the original drawing. Then place the canvas over the drawing; use a waterproof marker to trace directly onto the canvas.

Embroidery patterns are easily transferred onto fabric with a transfer pen. Trace the design onto paper and then invert the paper and rub the design onto the fabric. Iron-on transfer pencils are also available to apply patterns to fabric by ironing the tracing you make with the pencil from the paper onto the fabric. When making the transfer, make sure you trace the mirror image with the transfer pen or pencil to get a positive image.

Quilting patterns are drawn directly on the fabric (see directions for the *Mythical Beast Appliqué Quilt*).

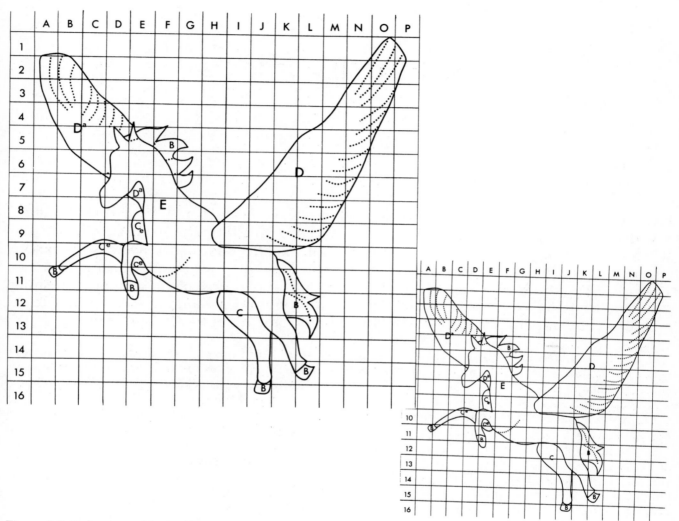

Figure 2-9. Enlarging with a grid.

CHAPTER THREE

Finishing Hints

Finishing can be the crucial step toward happiness or disgust with your final product. Always steam or press needlework face down to prevent flattening your stitches. Cross-stitch and quilting are good things to start with if you haven't finished needlework before because they are similar to working with lighter weight fabrics. Any seamstress can attempt cross-stitch finishing without fear. Regardless of my feelings about finishing needlepoint, I don't want to discourage those ambitious people among you who like to do projects from start to finish, so the following are some hints to get started.

Use only a mild soap to wash needlework. Treat it like a fine wool garment. I find that Ivory Snow is the best soap.

Never place your iron directly on the needlework. Always place a cloth between the iron and the needlework.

To steam (steam, rather than press when you are worried about color fastness or if you don't want to flatten your stitches) a piece of needlework either press with the cloth damp or hold the steam iron several inches above the needlework and push the steam button.

Always baste seams first. The large basting stitches are easier to rip than the more permanent stitching.

Use the appropriate sewing machine needle for the fabric weight you are finishing.

Press the seams after each step to prevent puckering or catching the seams in the next step.

BLOCKING NEEDLEPOINT

Most needlepoint needs some straightening after all the stitching has been completed and before it has been made into a finished product. Body oil that rubs off from your hands during stitching and any dirt that has accumulated needs to be removed before blocking. Blocking requires some strength, but it is not difficult.

Materials
- Plywood (larger than the piece to be blocked)
- Carpet tacks (rustproof)
- Brown paper (a brown paper bag opened out flat is suitable)
- Tack hammer
- Ruler
- Pencil
- Mild soap (*not* detergent)
- Towel

Directions
Measure the needlepoint to determine its outside dimensions. It is important to leave 1½ to 2 inches (4 to 5cm) of unworked canvas around the needlepoint for placing tacks later.

On brown paper, with pencil and ruler, draw a square or rectangle using these dimensions. Mark the center of each side on the brown paper pattern.

Soak the needlepoint in a mild soap solution in

cold water. Rinse out soap thoroughly but gently. Roll the needlepoint in a towel to remove excess water.

Tack the brown paper pattern to the plywood.

Place the needlepoint face down on the pattern and, starting at the center of one side of the needlepoint, tack the unworked canvas area to the plywood and brown paper. Make sure the needlepoint edge lines up with the line drawn on the brown paper. Repeat with the center of each of the other three sides. Keep the tack 1 inch (2.5cm) away from the stitching.

Stretching out from the center of each side, tack every 1/2 inch (1cm) until the sides are tacked to the corners. Work around the canvas so that each side is stretched consistently and equally out from the center.

Let the canvas dry completely before removing the needlepoint from the board. Do *not* remove the needlepoint from the board until you are ready to assemble the finished product.

If you are afraid to wet the needlepoint completely, use the steamer on your iron after you have stretched it while dry or mist it lightly with a sprayer.

Some needlepoints are so out of shape that this process will need to be repeated to get it completely square.

BLOCKING CROSS-STITCH AND BLACKWORK

Generally, counted cross-stitch and blackwork hold their shape during stitching. They require only washing and light pressing.

FINISHING STITCHES

These stitches are used mainly in the finishing of the projects in this book. They do have other purposes. The ladder stitch and whipstitch are used for appliqué and the herringbone is also used for embroidery. They are interchangeable in the finishing process but I have recommended which stitch seems to work best for which step.

Ladder Stitch

The ladder stitch is worked on the front sides of the pieces that are being joined. Start with the edges of the fabric or canvas next to each other face up towards you.

Knot your thread securely to the back of one piece and pull it to the front of that side on the stitching line.

Make your stitches where you want the two pieces to meet. Work back and forth between the two pieces in the sequence shown in Figure 3-3.

The stitches should be small on finer fabrics (1/8 inch) and larger on the coarser fabrics such as canvas.

As you work, pull in tightly to turn selvage under, bring the two pieces together snugly and hide the stitches. The stitching thread should not show on the front of your work. (Figure 3-3 is shown for clarity, not technique.)

Secure your ending thread and hide in the pillow or fabric by pulling the thread through from the ending stitch, into the back or inside, and then to the outside again approximately 1 inch (2.5cm) away from last stitch. Clip the thread close to your work while maintaining tension on the thread. It should disappear when cut.

Whipstitch

The whipstitch is worked in a continuous spiral joining edges of fabric, canvas, or yarn braid to each other. Start with the pieces to be joined in the position you want them to be in when the stitching is done.

Knot your thread in the back of the sturdiest piece and pull to the front of that piece.

What you are joining determines where you make your stitches. The main object is to have as little of the stitch showing as possible. Be sure to take tiny stitches in the edge of the fabric that will show on the outside. Catch only a little bit of the inside threads of a yarn braid when attaching it to a pillow edge, and only a bit of the fabric on the seam of the pillow.

Herringbone Stitch

The herringbone stitch is an elongated cross-stitch that gives a nice finished look when tacking a piece of fabric to the back of your wall hanging.

Knot your thread and secure it in the hemmed edge of your backing fabric. Pull it through to the stitching line on the front of the backing fabric.

The stitches should catch only the back of the needlepoint canvas and the backing fabric. Be careful not to have your stitches show on the front of the needlepoint. This stitch is decorative so do it as evenly as possible.

Hide the end of your thread between the needlepoint and backing fabric in the same way mentioned in the ladder stitch.

PILLOW FINISHING

Regardless of how beautiful your stitches look, if your pillow isn't finished properly the project will be spoiled. Follow these directions for professional results.

The fabric you use for the backing should be comparable in weight to the finished needlework. For example, use a heavier weight fabric, such as corduroy or velveteen, for needlepoint on canvas, but use a lighter weight fabric, such as broadcloth, for cross-stitch. I find that stretch fabrics don't work as well as the nonstretchable fabrics.

Materials
○ Backing fabric
○ Pillow form (or muslin and stuffing)
○ Cord (to make piping) or yarn (to make braid)
○ Curved needle

Directions for a Knife-Edge Pillow
Cut backing fabric the size of the needlework plus 2 inches (5cm). For knife-edge pillows with fabric piping, you will need 1 yard (1m) of the backing fabric.

Trim the needlework canvas so that approximately 8 unworked threads are left around the margin of the design after it is blocked. For needlework on fabric, leave ½ inch.

To make the piping, cut strips 2 inches (5cm) wide along the bias of the fabric (cut at a 45° angle to the selvage). To connect two pieces, overlap them—perpendicular to each other—at one end. Sew a seam at a 45° angle to across the intersection. Straighten out and press the seam flat. Cut the cord for the piping the desired length—2 inches (5cm) longer than the distance around the pillow. Fold the fabric strip, wrong sides together, over the cord and pin. Machine-baste as close to the cord as possible, without catching the cord with the thread.

Baste the piping to the needlework between the first and second rows of the needlepoint (around the circumference of other needlework). The rough edge should be on the outside; the basting line of the piping should be along the stitching line. Round the corners slightly when basting, and either cross the piping at the ends or tuck one end into the other where they meet.

With right sides together, baste the backing fabric to the needlework along the piping-to-needlework basting line. Starting 2 inches (5cm) before one corner and finishing 2 inches (5cm) after the last corner (thus leaving one side open), sew with a permanent stitch. Turn right side out. Make or buy a pillow form 2 inches (5cm) larger than the fin-

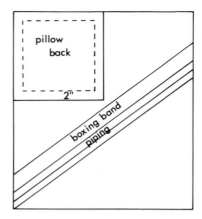

Figure 3-1. Basic cutting plan for knife-edged and boxed pillows, showing position of pillow back, piping and boxing band. The boxing band can be cut on the bias (as shown) or along the length of the fabric.

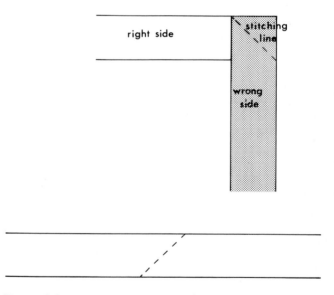

Figure 3-2. Connect two pieces of piping to make longer lengths.

ished needlework pillow. Insert into the pillow cover and adjust corners. Use the ladder stitch (Figure 3-3) and a curved needle to stitch the opening closed.

If you are applying a yarn braid (see directions below), leave a small opening to hide the ends.

Whipstitch (Figure 3-4) the yarn braid to the edge of the pillow. Hide ends in the small opening and use the ladder stitch to sew the opening closed.

Directions for a Box-Edge Pillow
Cut the fabric for the pillow back 2 inches (5cm) larger than the desired size. You will need 1½

20

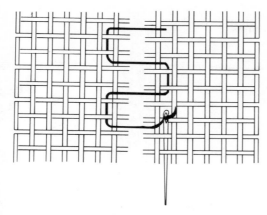

Figure 3-3. Ladder stitch shown connecting two pieces of canvas laid side by side. Pull the stitches tight so the edges come together, the selvage tucks under, and the stitches do not show.

yards (1.5m) of the backing fabric for the boxing band, piping, and pillow back.

Cut the boxing band 1 inch (2.5cm) longer than the perimeter of the pillow by 2 or 3 inches (5 or 7.5 cm) wide. (The width is a matter of personal preference.)

Trim the needlework as for the knife-edge pillow
Make piping, if desired .

Baste one length of piping to the needlework and one length of piping to the pillow back as for the knife-edge pillow.

Sew the ends of the boxing band together (take a ½-inch seam). Baste the band to the pillow top, along previous basting. Then baste the band to the pillow back, along previous basting. Sew pillow top and boxing band with a permanent stitch. Leaving one side open (as in knife-edge pillow), sew pillow back and boxing band with a permanent stitch. Turn right side out.

Insert pillow form and sew the opening closed.

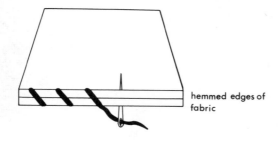

hemmed edges of fabric

Figure 3-4. Whipstitch: Take tiny stitches to catch the outside edges.

MAKING A WALL HANGING

Making a wall hanging out of your needlework is a nice way to display your projects without the formality of a frame.

Materials
- Fabric for backing and loops
- Interfacing
- Yarn for braid twist
- Dowel for hanging

Directions
Block the needlepoint and trim around the edge leaving ½ inch (1cm) of unworked threads or margin around the needlework design.

Fold a ½-inch (1cm) margin to the back of the needlework. Stitch down for needlepoint; press for cross-stitch.

To make loops, cut strips that are double the width and length you want the finished loops to be. Fold in half lengthwise, right sides together. Sew a ¼-inch seam along rough edge. Turn right side out. Press so that the seam is in the middle of the back side. Fold the strips in half; rough edges should meet, and the seam will be hidden. Baste rough edges together, and tack loops to the back of the needlework.

Cut backing fabric 1 inch (2.5cm) longer and wider than the finished needlework. Cut the interfacing slightly smaller than the finished needlework.

Whipstitch the interfacing to the back of the needlework around the edges.

Make a ½-inch (1cm) hem around the backing fabric by folding to the back ½ inch (1cm) and pressing. Clip or miter the corners so they will lie flat.

Using the herringbone stitch, stitch the backing fabric to the needlework around the edges. Leave about 2 inches (5cm) open in one side.

Whipstitch yarn braid (see directions below) around the outside edges of the needlework. Hide

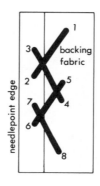

Figure 3-5. Herringbone stitch: Bring the needle up at 1, down at 2, up at 3 and so on. Do not go all the way through the front of the needlepoint but catch the back of the needlepoint with your needle to hold down the backing fabric.

the ends of the braid between the backing and the needlework. Flatten out the braid so that it doesn't make a lump, and use ladder or herringbone stitch to sew opening closed.

MAKING BRAID TWISTS FROM YARN

Instead of piping, yarn or floss can make a beautiful edge for your projects. A couple of hints: before making a full length of braid, experiment with short pieces of yarn to determine the number of plies or strands you need to get the thickness you want. Before twisting, the yarn should be approximately three times as long as the finished braid. Also, for long braids, two people will make the twisting easier; however, you can just as easily loop one end over a doorknob.

Directions

Fold the yarn in half and tie a knot to hold the two ends. Put the loop over a doorknob or something similar—you want the loop to stay put without slipping. Start twisting the knotted end (place your fingers or a pencil in the loop formed by the knot) until the yarn twists back on itself when tension is released.

Fold the yarn in half again, straightening out the twists until the braid is evenly twisted. Slip the knotted end through the loop at the doorknob end to keep the braid from untwisting. You can also tie a knot at this end for extra security.

Figure 3-7. Start twisting the knotted end until yarn twists back on itself.

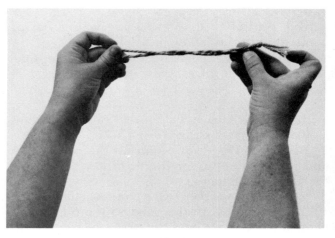

Figure 3-8. Fold yarn in half again.

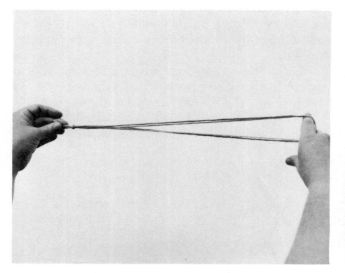

Figure 3-6. Fold yarn in half and tie a knot to hold the two ends.

Figure 3-9. Pull the end through the loop to keep the braid from untwisting.

FRAMING NEEDLEWORK

Putting your needlework in a frame under glass will preserve your work for future generations.

Materials

- Mediumweight white cardboard (for cross-stitch projects)
- Lightweight wood, approximately ¼-inch thick, or artist stretcher bars (for needlepoint projects)
- Batting
- Staple gun
- White glue
- Mat board
- Frame
- Glass (I prefer not to use glass because it makes the needlework harder to see but the choice is yours)

Directions

Cut the board to the dimensions of the finished needlework.

Cut batting slightly larger than the board and staple it in a few places around the raw edge of the board to hold the batting in place.

Center the needlework on the batting and, starting at the center edges, staple the piece to the raw edge of the board (*not* on the top). Work out toward the corners, stretching evenly.

You can glue cross-stitch to the back edge of the cardboard instead of using a staple gun, or you can lace it with string across the back.

Cut mat board to the size desired. Assemble with the needlework inside the frame.

If you put glass in your frame, space it *above* the needlework with spacers available at art stores or framing shops so that the needlework itself does not touch the glass.

If you are stretching your needlepoint over stretcher bars, place a piece of cardboard and batting on top before you stretch your needlepoint on the bars.

MAIL ORDER FINISHING

If you are concerned about the delicacy of your work or the difficulty of framing, have a professional frame the project. Most needlework shops offer finishing services or can recommend someone nearby who does finishing. Don't be afraid to ask to see samples of their work before commissioning them.

Needlework Framing and Finishing

Modern Needlepoint Mounting Co.
(send for brochure)
11 West 32 Street
New York, NY 10001

The Ugly Duckling Art Needlework Shop
700 Welch Road
Palo Alto, CA 94305

Finishing Only

The Knittery
2040 Union Street
San Francisco, CA 94123

Needlecraft House
Main Street
West Townsend, MA 01474

CHAPTER FOUR

Chinatown Dragon Needlepoint Pillow

When I was asked by the San Francisco Embroiderer's Guild of America to design a dragon for their San Francisco bicentennial rug, I searched for pictures of dragons to give me an idea of what Chinese dragons looked like. The face of this dragon was inspired by a Ming Dynasty bowl. The size square for the rug required by the Guild determined the shape of the dragon's body. This was my very first design and has inspired all my other dragon stitching adventures. This pillow, from that rug design, measures 16 by 12 inches (41 by 30.5cm).

MATERIALS

- #14 mono canvas, 20 by 16 inches (51 by 41cm)
- Paternayan Persian yarn. See Color Chart (Figure 4-2)
- Tapestry needle # 20
- Gray marker
- Fabric for backing (see *Finishing Hints*)
- Yarn braid—Paternayan Persian #510 (see *Finishing Hints*)

DIRECTIONS

1. Refer to Figures 4-2A and B. The design measures 221 threads by 187 threads.
2. Tape edges of canvas with masking tape.
3. Lightly mark a 2-inch (5cm) margin around the edge with a gray marker.
4. Find the center of the design by following the arrows at the edges of the chart. The dragon, pagoda, and background are worked in tent stitch (basketweave or continental stitch). Use 2 plies of the Persian yarn for these stitches. Start stitching the pagoda arm nearest the center point. Work out to the edges of the design until dragon, pagoda, and cloud flowers are finished.

5. To make the dragon body easier, stitch scale lines first, then fill in with surrounding colors. To avoid miscounting, do *not* try to stitch all of the scale lines at one time. There is a separate chart (Figure 4-3) of the scale lines to make them clearer. Put in the yellow fins that overlap body before filling in the colors surrounding the fins. Tweeding (SS and AA on chart) is done by using 1 ply of each color to give a more gradual gradation of color.
6. Do the bargello border before filling in the background with basketweave (see Figures 4-4 and 4-5). Use 3 plies of the Persian yarn for the bargello stitch. This border is 4-way bargello—the top and the bottom of the border is stitched vertically, the sides of the border are stitched horizontally. Work the bargello stitch out from the center toward the corners. The bargello stitch is worked over 4 threads except at the corners where the stitches need to be longer and shorter to compensate for the change in direction of 90°. No stitch is longer than over 5 canvas threads. Use a pencil or gray marker to draw a diagonal line through the corner as a reference (see border graph—Figure 4-5).
7. When border colors are complete, fill in with background color to the edge of the design with a

Figure 4-1A. Chinatown Dragon—stitched by the author.

Figure 4-1B. Chinatown Dragon in cross-stitch—stitched by Colleen Fairbairn.

Figure 4-2. Chinatown Dragon chart.

Code	Color	# of Strands	Design Part
	Paternayan Persian yarn, 33-inch (84-cm) strands		
■	#840 dark salmon	10 strands	darkest
· ·	#841 salmon	40 strands	border
ss	#841, #821 tweed		dragon
xx	#821 tangerine	40 strands	border, body
AA	#821, #800 tweed		
=	#800 dark marigold	27 strands	border
oo	#843 light salmon	10 strands	
III	#802 marigold	2 strands	lightest
++	#353 fuchsia	26 strands	border, feet, cloud flower
CC	#510 dark old blue	32 strands	border, pagoda
	#503 federal blue	193 strands	border, background
	#772 sunny yellow	15 strands	fins, mouth, eyes
//	#751 old gold	15 strands	scales
⊠	#261 white	1 strand	teeth
⊠	#693 loden green	1 strand	eye pupil

26

Figure 4-2A

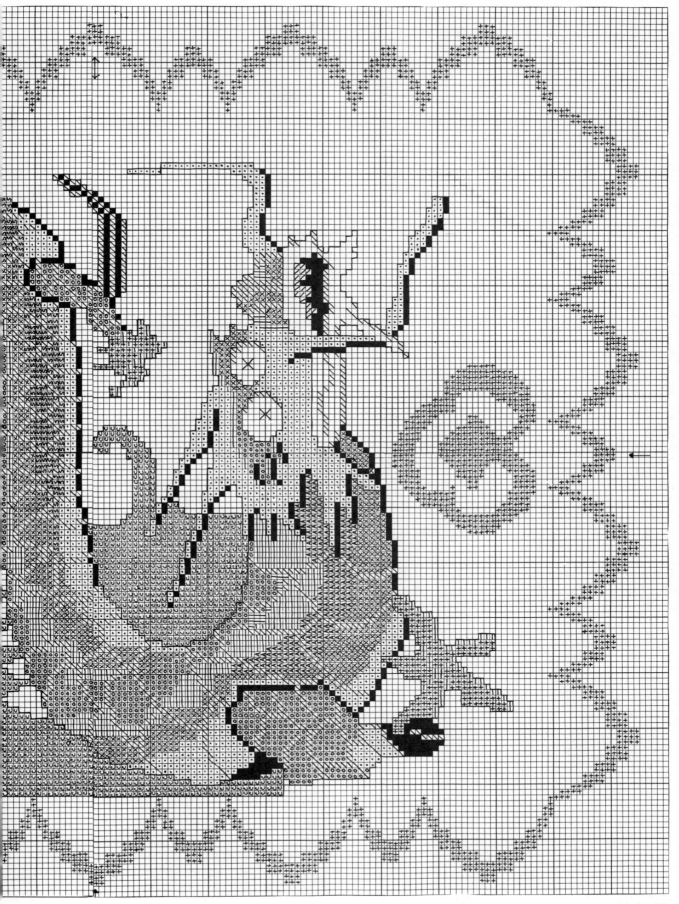

Figure 4-2B

bargello stitch. To make a straight edge, take shorter stitches to fill in the last row (see Figure 4-6 of bargello corner to see how shorter compensating stitches make a straight edge around the pillow).

8. Fill in background around design and inside of border with basketweave stitch.

9. Block the design and finish into a knife-edge pillow with braid trim (see *Finishing Hints*).

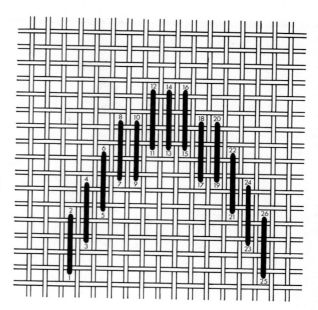

Figure 4-4. Bargello stitch sequence.

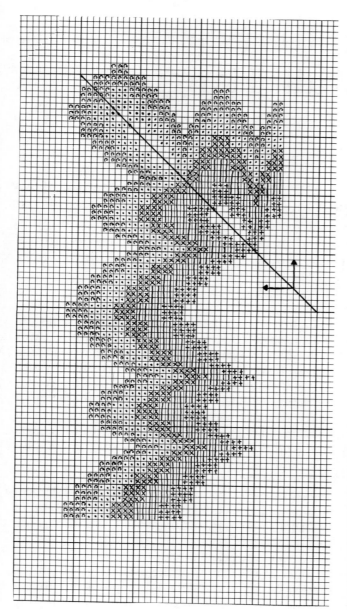

Figure 4-5. Bargello border chart.

Figure 4-3. Detail of dragon scales. *Opposite page.*

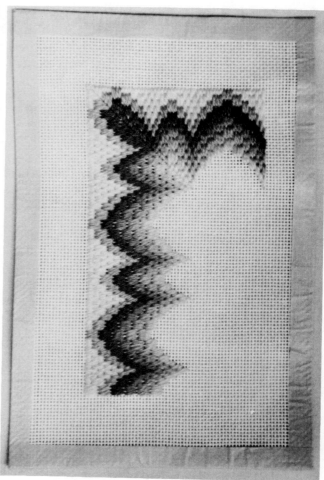

Figure 4-6. Bargello border and corner.

CHAPTER FIVE

Dragon in the Sea
Needlepoint Wall Hanging

This dragon was inspired by a Japanese cloisonné vase that sits on the mantle at my aunt's house. I took slides of the different aspects of the vase; then projected the slides on the wall and made the drawings. The drawings were expanded to make a rectangular wall hanging. Cotton and wool threads were used in this design to give contrast in texture between the dragon, spray, waves, and background. The finished wall hanging measures 17 by 22 inches (43 by 56cm).

MATERIALS

- #18 mono canvas, 21 by 26 inches (53.5 by 66cm)
- Paternayan Persian yarn. See Color Chart (Figure 5-2)
- DMC embroidery floss. See Color Chart (Figure 5-2)
- DMC Perle cotton, size 5. See Color Chart (Figure 5-2)
- Tapestry needle #22
- Gray marker
- Liquitex Acrylic Paint, black (optional)
- Fabric for backing (see *Finishing Hints*)
- Yarn braid—Paternayan Persian #570 (see *Finishing Hints*)
- ¾-inch (1.5cm) dowel, 23 inches (58.5cm) long
- Two ¾-inch (1.5cm) wood knobs
- White glue
- Spray enamel, black

DIRECTIONS

1. Refer to Figures 5-2A through H. The design measures 401 by 308 threads.
2. Tape the edges of the canvas with masking tape.
3. Lightly mark a 2-inch (5cm) margin around the edge with a gray marker. Dilute Liquitex paint with water and paint the background portion of the canvas. If you prefer, stain the entire canvas by dipping it in a tub of strong cold tea. This will prevent the white canvas threads from showing through under the dark background.
4. Each chart overlaps 10 stitches with the charts on the other pages. The schematic diagram (Figure 5-3) shows how they are all assembled.
5. The entire design is stitched in tent stitch (basketweave or continental). Use 1 ply of Persian wool, 6 plies of embroidery floss, and 1 strand of Perle cotton. (When working with #18 canvas, I use shorter strands because the single ply frays more easily than a thicker thread.)
6. Start at the center of the design and stitch the dragon. Refer to the detailed graph of the dragon head (Figure 5-4) to prevent confusion, since the dragon head appears on graph B and continues on graph C.
7. Outline the waves with the darkest federal blue before filling in with other colors. Don't try to do all the outlining at one time. Fill in the lighter colors gradually as you stitch the design.

Figure 5-1. Dragon in the Sea—stitched by the author.

8. Stitch in white spray before filling in with pale blue floss and federal blue shades.

9. Fill in spray droplets after the background has been stitched around the drops.

10. Block the completed design, back with fabric, make and sew on fabric loops, and edge with braid of background color (see *Finishing Hints*).

11. Glue knobs to the ends of the dowel.

12. When glue is dry, hang the dowel with sewing thread at both ends. Spray with black enamel paint. Let dry.

13. Insert black dowel through fabric loops and hang needlepoint.

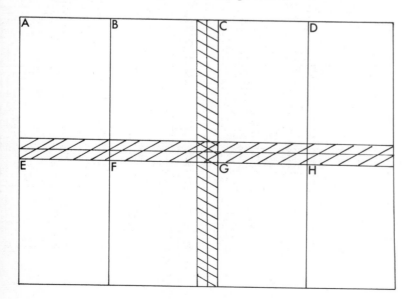

Figure 5-3. Diagram of overlapping threads on chart. Slashes indicate the overlapping areas. The charts overlap each other by 10 threads.

Figure 5-2. Dragon in the Sea chart.

Code	Color	# of Strands	Design Part
Paternayan Persian yarn, 33-inch (84-cm) strands			
■	#500 darkest federal blue	60 strands	waves
XX	#502 dark federal blue	10 strands	waves
//	#503 federal blue	46 strands	waves
CC	#504 medium federal blue	40 strands	waves
++	#505 light federal blue	30 strands	waves
OO	#506 pale federal blue	10 strands	waves
	#570 dark navy blue	152 strands	background
DMC embroidery floss, 8-meter skeins			
SS	#995 dark electric blue	4 skeins	dragon body
VV	#996 electric blue	5 skeins	dragon body
**	#519 light sky blue	1 skein	dragon body
▭	#726 light topaz	1 skein	iris of eye
X	#310 black	1 skein	pupil of eye
II	#606 bright orange red	2 skeins	tendrils
PP	#926 dark gray-green	1 skein	tendrils
▲▲	#975 dark golden brown	1 skein	eyebrows, tendrils
▭	#775 light baby blue	6 skeins	spray
XX	#415 pearl gray	1 skein	whiskers
DMC perle cotton, size 5, 25-meter skeins			
··	white	2 skeins	spray
=	ecru	2 skeins	whiskers, tummy
TT	#976 medium gold-brown	1 skein	tummy, horns
YY	#498 Christmas red	1 skein	tendrils
NN	#321 Christmas red	1 skein	tendrils
SS	#699 Christmas green	2 skeins	back fins

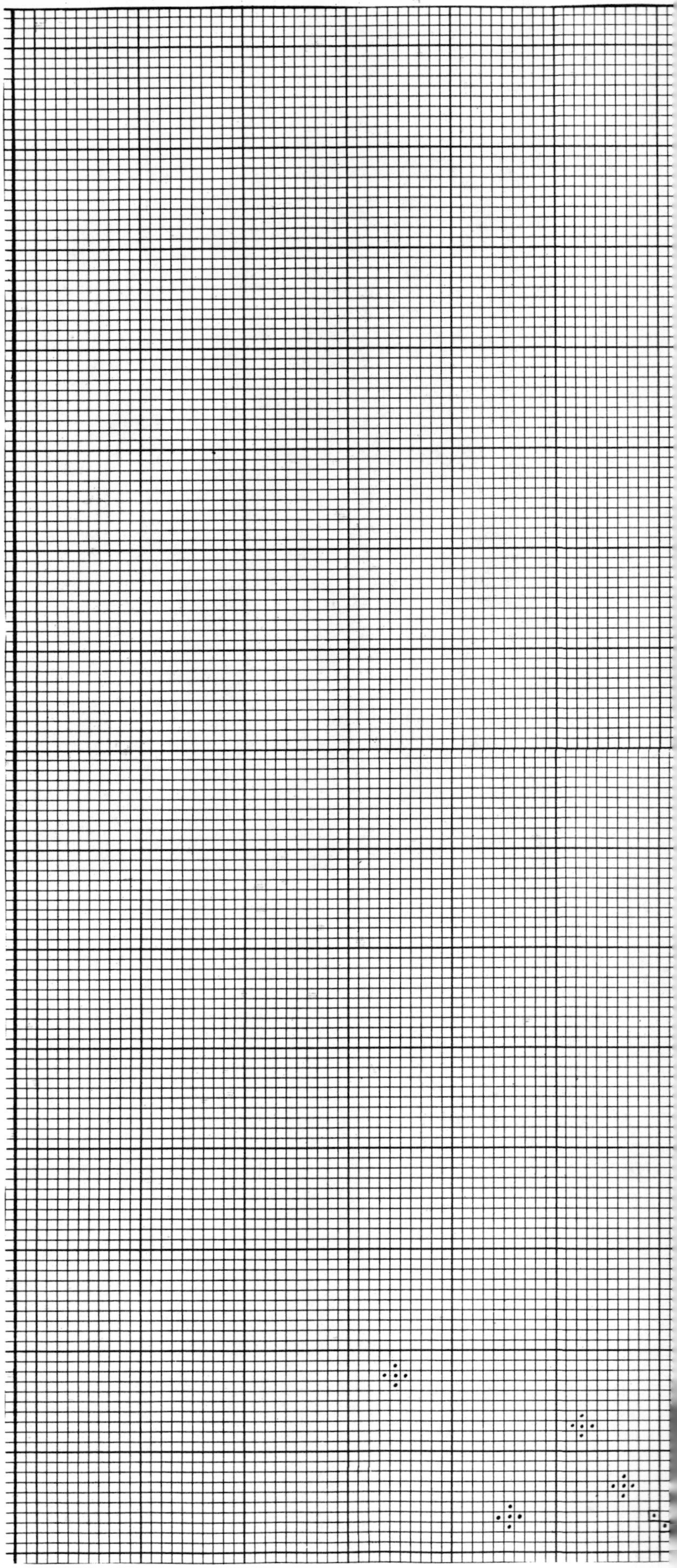

Figure 5-2A

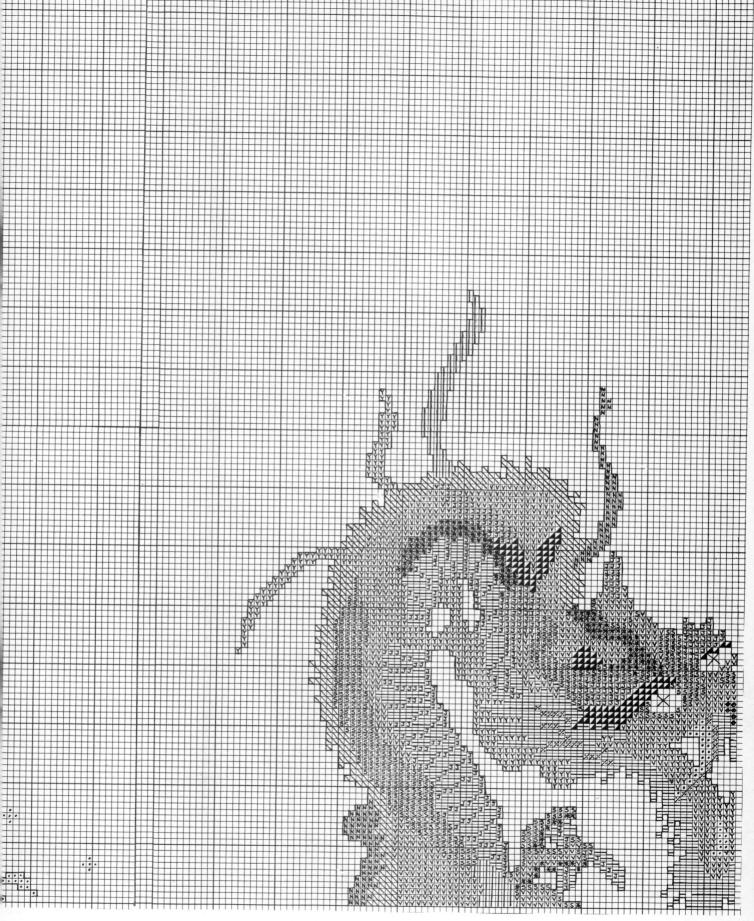

Figure 5-2B

Figure 5-2C

34

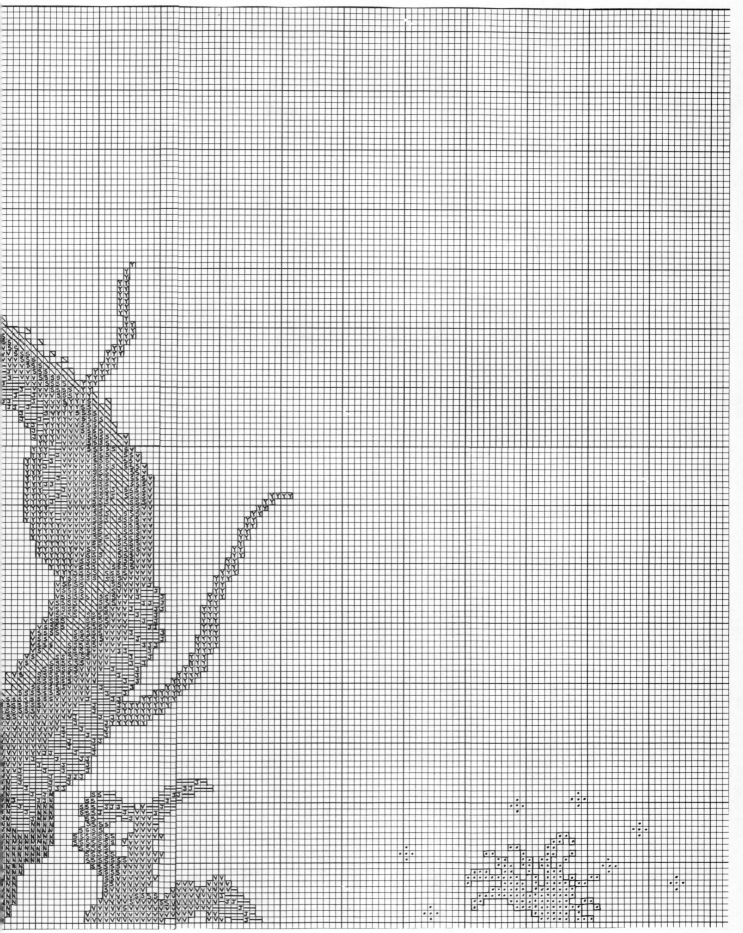

Figure 5-2D

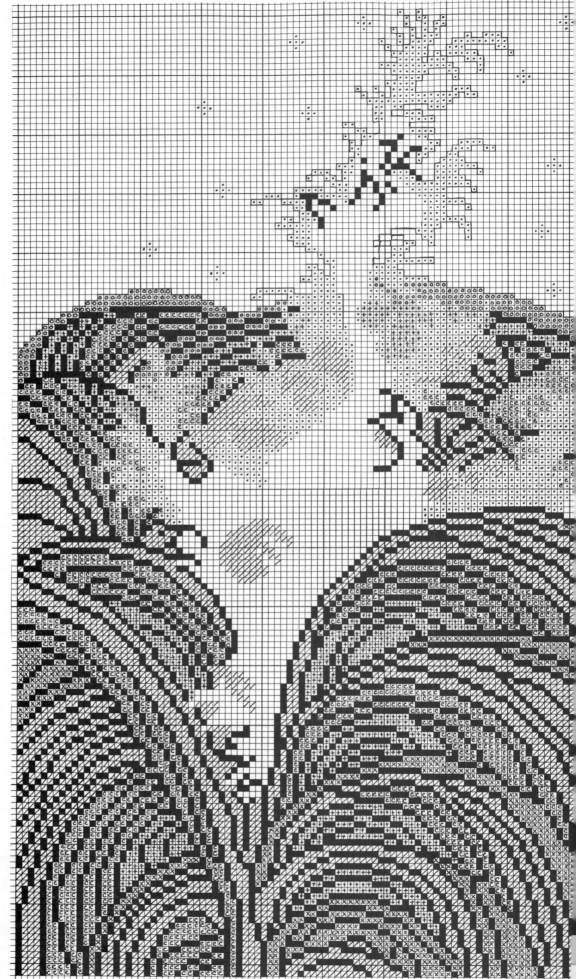

Figure 5-2E

Figure 5-2F

Figure 5-2G

Figure 5-2H

Figure 5-4. Detail of dragon's face.

CHAPTER SIX

Unicorn and Griffin Needlepoint Pillows

The unicorn and the griffin designs shown in Figure 6-1 are adaptations from medieval tapestries. The unicorn was a beautiful and elusive creature, while the griffin was ferocious. Both were used for heraldic crests and tapestry designs and are still being used to represent products and places. The border design in this piece is a simplification of the background woven in the original griffin tapestry. I have used different textured threads, cotton and wool, to make the characters stand out from the background. Each pillow measures 15 by 15 inches (38 by 38cm).

UNICORN PILLOW MATERIALS

- ○ #14 mono canvas, 19 by 19 inches (48.5 by 48.5 cm)
- ○ DMC Perle cotton, size 3. See Color Chart (Figure 6-2)
- ○ Paternayan Persian yarn. See Color Chart (Figure 6-2)
- ○ Balger #16 metallic. See Color Chart (Figure 6-2)
- ○ Tapestry needle #20
- ○ Gray marker
- ○ Fabric for backing (see *Finishing Hints*)
- ○ Yarn braid—Paternayan Persian #660 (see *Finishing Hints*)

GRIFFIN PILLOW MATERIALS

- ○ #14 mono canvas, 19 by 19 inches (48.5 by 48.5 cm)
- ○ DMC Perle cotton, size 3. See Color Chart (Figure 6-4)
- ○ Paternayan Persian yarn. See Color Chart (Figure 6-4)
- ○ Tapestry needle #20
- ○ Gray marker
- ○ Fabric for backing (see *Finishing Hints*)
- ○ Yarn braid—Paternayan Persian Yarn #660 (see *Finishing Hints*)

Figure 6-1. Unicorn—stitched by Elizabeth Lucasi and Leslie Armistead.

Figure 6-3. Griffin—stitched by Elizabeth Lucasi.

Figure 6-2. Unicorn chart.

Code	Color	# of Strands	Design Part
DMC perle cotton, size #3, 15-meter skeins			
⟨⟨white dots⟩⟩	white	4 skeins	body
⟨⟨XX⟩⟩	#762 very light pearl gray	1 skein	body
⟨⟨solid⟩⟩	#413 dark pewter gray	1 skein	eye, mouth, hooves
⟨⟨cc⟩⟩	#822 light beige-gray	1 skein	body, horn
⟨⟨//⟩⟩	#783 gold	1 skein	collar, hooves
⟨⟨∞⟩⟩	#797 royal blue	1 skein	collar
Paternayan Persian yarn, 33-inch (84-cm) strands			
⟨⟨shaded⟩⟩	#660 dark pine green	225 strands	background
⟨⟨\\\⟩⟩	#662 pine green	25 strands	border
⟨⟨ss⟩⟩	#694 light loden green	25 strands	border
Balger #16 metallic, 10-meter skeins			
⟨⟨XX⟩⟩	#032 pearl	1 skein	horn

Figure 6-2A

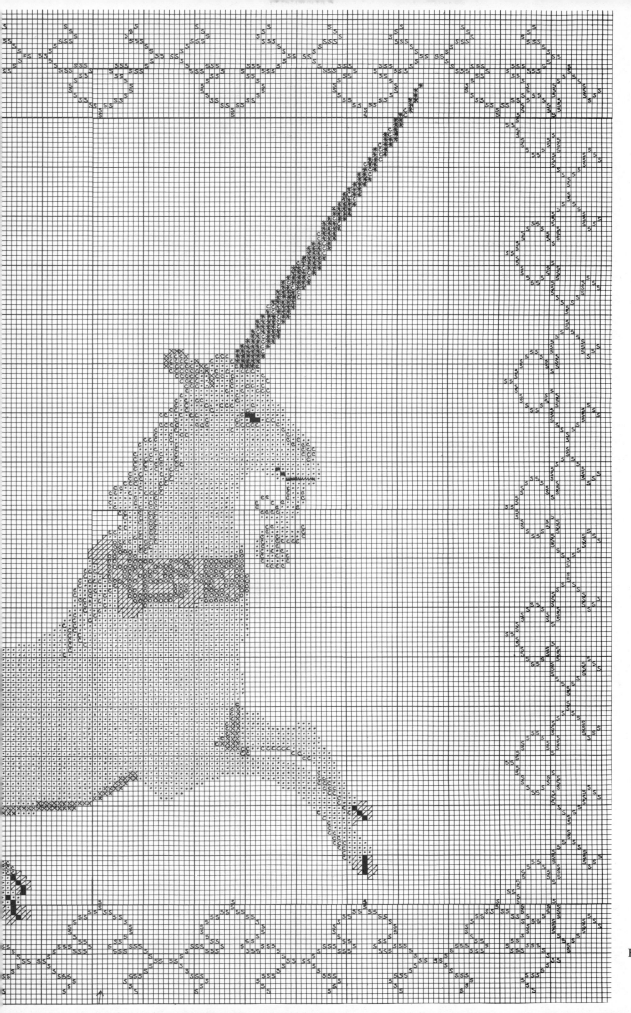

Figure 6-2B

Figure 6-4. Griffin chart.

Code	Color	# of Skeins	Design Part
DMC perle cotton, size 3, 15-meter skeins			
◢◢	#918 dark brick red	1 skein	feathers
zz	#666 bright Christmas red	1 skein	feathers
⊢⊢	#606 bright orange-red	1 skein	feathers
oo	#608 bright orange	1 skein	feathers, tongue
∕∕	#971 pumpkin	1 skein	feathers
··	#726 light topaz	1 skein	feathers, beak, feet, tail
XX	#783 gold	1 skein	lion body, claws, beak
═	#434 light brown	1 skein	lion body
✳✳	#300 very dark mahogany	1 skein	lion body
$$	#898 very coffee brown	1 skein	lion body, claws
■	#310 black	1 skein	eye, nostrils, feet
⊓⊓	#472 ultra-light avocado green	1 skein	claws
Paternayan Persian yarn, 33-inch (84-cm) strands			
	#660 dark pine green	225 strands	background
◥◥	#662 pine green	25 strands	border
ss	#694 light loden green	25 strands	border

Figure 6-4A

Figure 6-4B

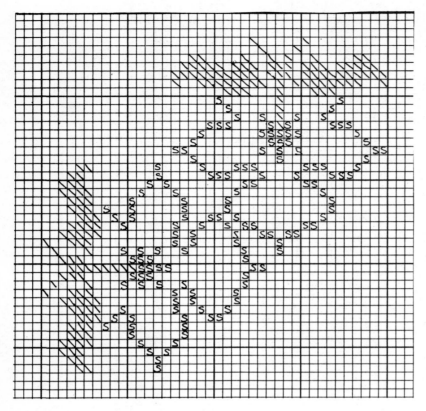

Figure 6-5. Border chart.

DIRECTIONS FOR BOTH PILLOWS

1. Refer to Figure 6-2 and Figures 6-4A and B. The designs measure 217 threads by 217 threads.
2. Tape the edges of the canvas with masking tape.
3. Lightly mark a 2-inch (5cm) margin around the edge of the canvas with a gray marker.
4. By looking at the border pattern, pick out the center of the middle motif and stitch the border design out toward the corners and around the edges. The entire design is worked in tent stitch. Use 1 strand of Perle cotton and 2 plies of Persian yarn. Check your counting several times to catch any mistakes.
5. Stitch the animal starting near the border or in the center of the canvas.
6. Fill in the background (see detail chart—Figure 6-5) adding 3 rows of background color around the outside of the border.
7. Block, assemble into a pillow, and sew on yarn braid to the pillow edge.

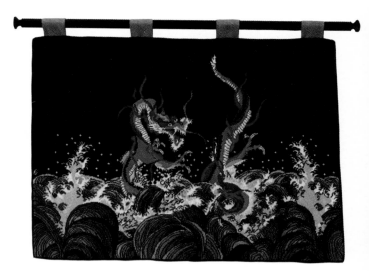

Above: Dragon in the Sea Picture

Upper right: Dragon in the Sea wall hanging

Lower right: Chinatown Dragon pillow, Medieval
Griffin pillow, and Unicorn pillow

Left: Phoenix wall hanging and Enchanted Land pillow

Above: Taiyuin pillow, "C" pillow, Pegasus box

Below: Blackwork Dragon picture, Blackwork Phoenix picture, and Heracles and Achelous pillow

elow: Mythical Character Alphabet wall hanging

Right: Pegasus purse

Below: Mythical Beast Quilt

CHAPTER SEVEN

Enchanted Land Needlepoint Pillow and Phoenix Needlepoint Wall Hanging

The phoenix represents rebirth. The legend says that at the death of the bird, it catches fire and a new phoenix rises from the ashes. The enchanted land is where this mythical bird lives. Both of these designs were adapted from one piece of Chinese silk embroidery. The original embroidery was photographed and drawings were made from slides projected on the wall. This is a relatively easy way to enlarge designs from the original source. The pillow and wall hanging have been stitched in wool with colors close to the original silk colors. The finished pillow measures 14 by 15 inches (35.5. by 38cm); the hanging measures 14 by 30 inches (35.5 by 76cm).

ENCHANTED LAND PILLOW MATERIALS
○ #14 mono canvas, 18 by 19 inches (46 by 48.5cm)
○ Paternayan Persian yarn. See Color Chart (Figure 7-2)
○ Tapestry needle #20
○ Gray marker
○ Fabric for backing and piping (see *Finishing Hints*)

DIRECTIONS FOR ENCHANTED LAND PILLOW

1. Refer to Figure 7-2. The design measures 221 threads by 228 threads.
2. Tape the edges of the canvas with masking tape.
3. Lightly mark a 2-inch (5cm) margin around the edge of the canvas with a gray marker.
4. Find the center of the design following the arrows at the edges of the chart. The design is worked in tent stitch with 2 plies of Persian yarn. Start stitching the leaf at the center. Stitch out to the edges until plants and fence are finished.

5. Stitch the #845 light salmon and #844 medium salmon stripes of the border (see Figure 7-5) in the positions indicated around center design. Be careful to overlap the stripes at the corners as shown in the diagram of the border; each corner is different. Stitch the butterflies around the edge (see charts, Figures 7-3 and 7-4). Be careful of the spacing differences on the edges of the border between the butterflies. Stitch the larger areas of the butterflies first, then stitch the small spots so you have something to tuck your ends into.
6. Fill in the background when the design is stitched, starting 3 rows beyond the border.
7. Block the design; finish into a knife-edge pillow.

PHOENIX WALL HANGING MATERIALS
○ #14 mono canvas, 18 by 34 inches (46 by 86.5cm)
○ Paternayan Persian yarn. See Color Chart (Figure 7-7)
○ Tapestry needle #20
○ Gray marker
○ Bamboo-style frame (see *Finishing Hints*)

Figure 7-1. Enchanted Land—stitched by Karen Benight.

DIRECTIONS FOR PHOENIX WALL HANGING

1. Refer to Figures 7-7A through F. The design measures 427 threads by 198 threads.
2. Tape the edges of the canvas with masking tape.
3. Lightly mark a 2-inch margin (5cm) around the edge of the canvas with a gray marker.
4. Find the center of the design by following the arrows at the edges of the middle chart. Use 2 plies of Persian yarn to stitch the entire design in tent stitch. Start stitching the bird leg near this center point and stitch out toward the edges. Each chart overlaps 5 stitches on all sides with the charts on the other pages (see Figure 7-8).
5. Fill in background when design is completed.
6. Block the design and frame (see *Finishing Hints*).

Figure 7-2. Enchanted Land chart.

Code	Color	# of Strands	Design P
Paternayan Persian yarn, 33-inch (84-cm) strands			
	#500 darkest federal blue	30 strands	leaves, butterf] fence
xx	#501 dark federal blue	15 strands	leaves, butterf]
cc	#503 medium federal blue	20 strands	leaves
11	#504 light federal blue	10 strands	leaves
✓✓	#680 dark peacock green	8 strands	flowers, butterf]
ss	#683 peacock green	8 strands	flowers
	#686 light peacock green	11 strands	flowers, butterf]
vv	#843 salmon	5 strands	flowers, butterf]
++	#844 medium salmon	10 strands	flowers, borders
∞	#845 light salmon	12 strands	flowers, borders
//	#846 pale salmon	6 strands	flowers
✓	#912 dark dusty pink	15 strands	butterflie fence
zz	#913 dusty pink	7 strands	fence, butterf]
//	#915 light dusty pink	4 strands	fence
··	#714 light mustard	25 strands	butterflie flowers leaves
**	#213 pearl gray	4 strands	fence
	#261 natural white	193 strands	backgrou

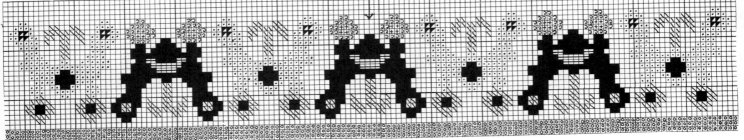

Figure 7-3. Chart of horizontal butterfly border.

Figure 7-4. Chart of vertical butterfly border.

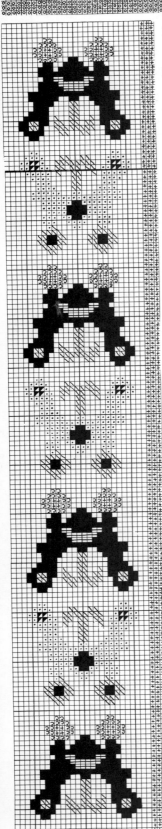

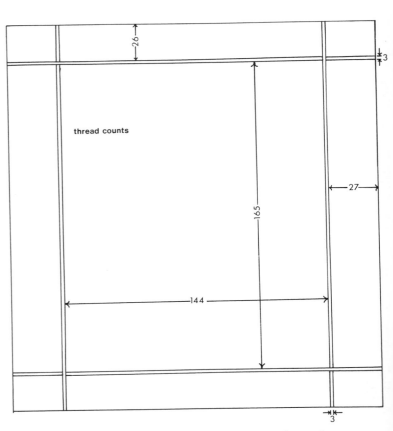

Figure 7-5. Diagram of border position and Enchanted Land design.

Figure 7-6. Phoenix—stitched by the author.

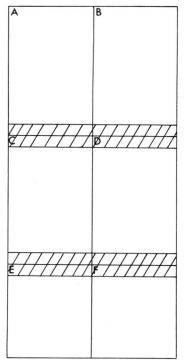

Figure 7-8. Diagram of overlapping threads on chart. Slashes indicate the overlapping areas. The charts overlap each other by 5 threads.

Figure 7-7. Phoenix chart.

Code	Color	# of Strands	Design Part
	Paternayan Persian yarn, 33-inch (84-cm) strands		
	#261 natural white	333 strands	background
	#500 darkest federal blue	45 strands	vegetation, feathers, swallows
	#501 dark federal blue	6 strands	vegetation
	#502 federal blue	20 strands	vegetation, feathers
	#503 medium federal blue	6 strands	vegetation
	#504 light federal blue	7 strands	vegetation
	#680 darkest peacock green	38 strands	vegetation, feathers
	#685 peacock green	4 strands	feathers
	#613 light hunter green	45 strands	vegetation, feathers
	#841 dark salmon	4 strands	feathers
	#843 salmon	5 strands	feathers, flowers
	#844 light salmon	4 strands	feathers, flowers
	#845 pale salmon	25 strands	feathers, flowers
	#730 dark honey gold	10 strands	feathers
	#741 dark tobacco	15 strands	feathers
	#744 light tobacco	10 strands	feathers
	#714 mustard	15 strands	vegetation, legs, beak, swallow
	#212 light pearl gray	5 strands	feathers
	#260 white	1 strand	eye
	#220 black	1 strand	eye, beak
	#912 dark dusty pink	2 strands	swallow
	#913 dusty pink	1 strand	swallow
	#915 pale dusty pink	2 strands	swallow

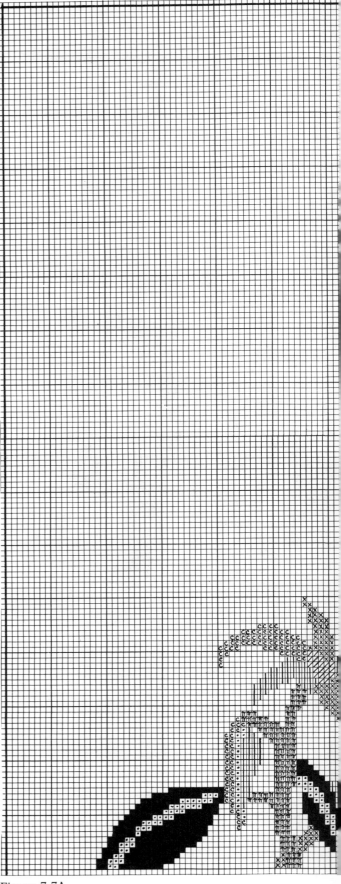

Figure 7-7A

Figure 7-7B

Figure 7-7C

Figure 7-7D

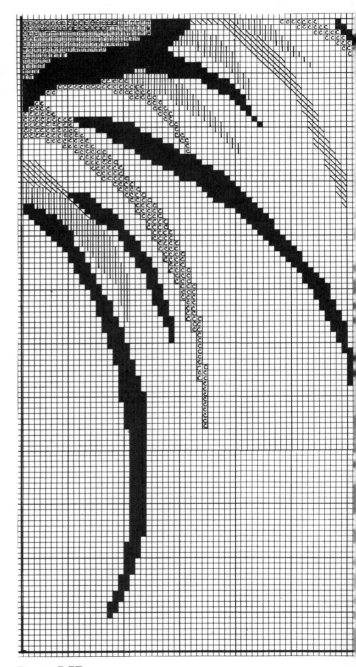

Figure 7-7E

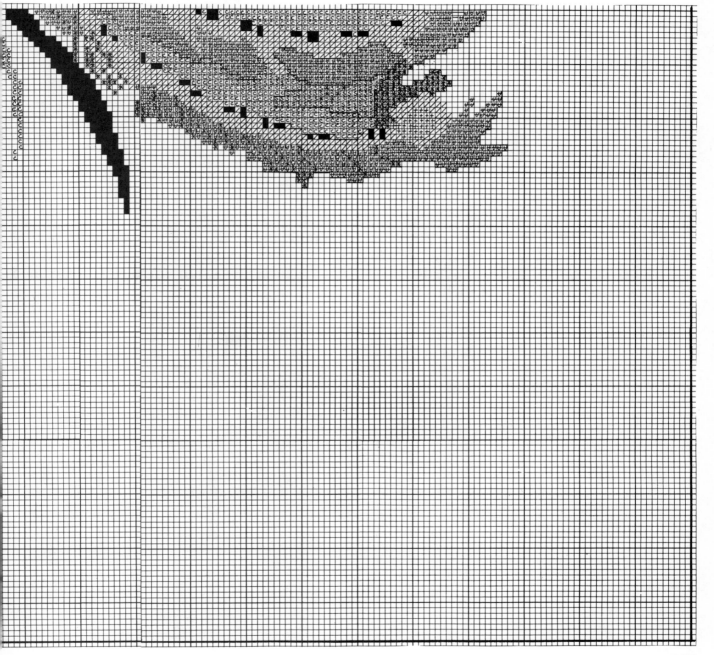

Figure 7-7F

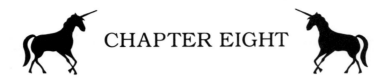

CHAPTER EIGHT

Taiyuin Needlepoint Pillow

This design was adapted from a painting in a temple in Nikko, Japan. The temples found in Nikko are very Chinese in style, and this creature is very similar to a Chinese Foo Lion. The taiyuin is a Japanese mythical beast with a ferocious countenance. The finished pillow measures 13 by 14 inches (33 by 36cm).

DIRECTIONS

- #14 mono canvas, 17 by 18 inches (43 by 46cm)
- Paternayan Persian yarn. See Color Chart (Figure 8-2)
- Tapestry needle #20
- Gray marker
- Fabric for box-edge pillow and piping (see *Finishing Hints*)

DIRECTIONS

1. Refer to Figures 8-2A and B. The design measures 182 threads by 196 threads.

2. Tape the edges of the canvas with masking tape.

3. Lightly mark a 2-inch (5cm) margin around the canvas edge with a gray marker.

4. Starting in the center, stitch out toward the edges of the design. The entire design is stitched in tent stitch with 2 plies of Persian yarn.

5. Starting in the upper right-hand corner, fill in the background with basketweave stitch.

6. Block the canvas and assemble into a box-edge pillow (see *Finishing Hints*).

Figure 8-1. Taiyuin—stitched by Leslie Armistead.

Figure 8-2. Taiyuin chart.

Code	Color	# of Strands	Design Part
		Paternayan Persian yarn, 33-inch (84-cm) strands	
	#655 light olive green	85 strands	background
	#503 medium federal blue	20 strands	body
	#754 light old gold	23 strands	tail, mane, tendrils
	#221 charcoal	10 strands	body, tail, mane, tendrils
	#213 light pearl gray	31 strands	body
	#612 hunter green	33 strands	tail, mane, tendrils

Figure 8-2A

Figure 8-2B

CHAPTER NINE

Cherry Blossom Flower Child Cross-Stitch Stationery Portfolio

Fairies appear in countless children's stories. Cicely Mary Baker looked to the gardens and wild flowers of England for inspiration for her flower fairies. My flower children were suggested by Japanese cherry blossoms and California poppies. This design arose from several different sources. When my husband and I were in Japan we saw a boy picking the blooms from a cherry tree. I used the slide we took of the boy for the design of the flower child. The cherry blossom branch was adapted from a porcelain vase that was used to ship tea from China. The wings were inspired by a butterfly. The finished design measures 7¼ by 8¼ inches (18.5 by 21cm); the finished stationery portfolio measures 10 by 12 inches (25.5 by 30.5cm).

MATERIALS

○ #18 Aida cloth, ivory, 12 by 11 inches (30.5 by 28cm)
○ DMC embroidery floss. See Color Chart (Figure 9-2)
○ Tapestry needle #26
○ Corduroy fabric, ½ yard (46cm)
○ Broadcloth, ½ yard (46cm) each of one solid color and one print
○ Interfacing, ½ yard (46cm)
○ Satin ribbon, ⅜ inch wide, 3 yards (3m)
○ 2 pieces heavy (noncorrugated) cardboard, 12 by 10 inches (30.5 by 25.5cm)
○ 2 pieces batting, 12 by 10 inches (30.5 by 25.5cm)
○ White glue
○ Curved needle

DIRECTIONS

1. Refer to Figure 9-2. The design measures 149 by 131 threads.

2. Zigzag around the edges of the fabric to prevent unraveling.

3. Starting in the center, cross-stitch the design out toward the edges. Use 2 plies of the embroidery floss for cross-stitches.

4. Backstitch around the flowers with 2 plies of #3688 fuchsia and around the wings with #3685 dark fuchsia. Backstitch around the tree branch in front of the wing with #3371 black-brown.

5. The anthers of the bloom are random straight stitches out from the center of the flower. Use 1 ply of #781 light brown to stitch the anthers.

6. Make French knots with 2 plies of #3688 fuchsia in the center of the flowers (for the pistils).

7. Wash. Press gently when dry.

8. Now you are ready to assemble the portfolio. Spread white glue on one side of each piece of cardboard. Place the batting on the glue and let it dry completely.

9. Cut a corduroy piece 13 by 22 inches (33 by 56cm). (I prefer that the wales, or ribs, of the corduroy run vertically on the portfolio.) On the

Figure 9-1. Cherry Blossom
Flower Child—stitched by
Kate Johnson.

Figure 9-3. Inside the
portfolio.

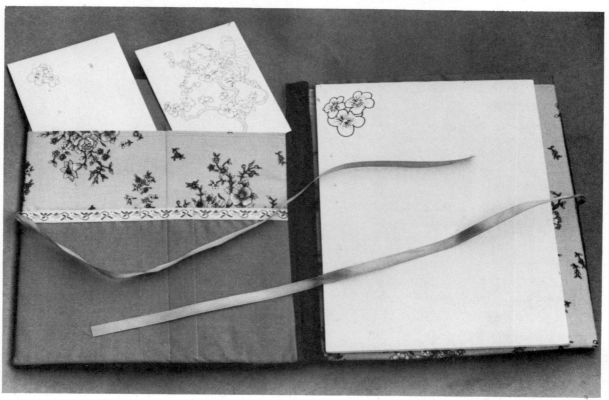

wrong side of the fabric, draw a window 7¹/₄ by 8¹/₄ inches (18.5 by 21cm). See Figure 10-3 for placement.

10. Cut a piece of solid color broadcloth 13 by 10 inches (33 by 25.5cm). With right sides together and edges matched, pin the broadcloth to the corduroy on the window side. Sew completely around the window on the drawn window lines. Cut out the window, leaving a ¹/₂-inch (1cm) seam. Clip in toward each corner. Turn the broadcloth toward the back of the corduroy. Press.

11. Pin the corduroy over the cross-stitch pattern, matching edges. Machine topstitch ¹/₄ inch (.5cm) from window edge on the corduroy around the window to hold the cross-stitch in place.

12. Pin the ribbon (see Figure 10-4) around the window, forming a frame and extending the lines out to the edges. Cut each ribbon at the edge of the fabric as it is pinned in place. Stitch the ribbon in place along each edge of the ribbon. Cut two ribbon pieces—each 18 inches (46cm) long—and attach to the center of the corduroy at each side edge.

13. Cut broadcloth as follows: two pieces of plain color, each 13 by 11 inches (33 by 28cm); one piece of print, 24 by 11 inches (1 by 28cm); one piece of print, 19 by 11 inches (48 by 28cm); one piece of print, 13 by 11 inches (33 by 28cm). Cut one piece of corduroy, 2 by 13 inches (5 by 33cm). Cut interfac-

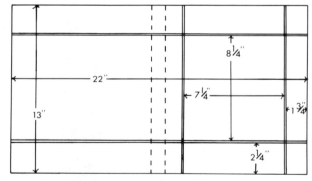

Figure 9-4. Measurements of portfolio outside.

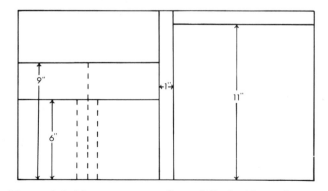

Figure 9-5. Measurements of portfolio inside pockets.

Figure 9-2. Cherry Blossom Flower Child chart.

Code	Color	# of Skeins	Design Part
DMC embroidery floss, 8-meter skeins			
▟▟	#3345 dark hunter green	1 skein	pants, wings, buds
∞	#3347 medium yellow green	1 skein	pants, wings, buds
	#781 dark topaz	1 skein	branches, wings
▮▮	#780 very dark topaz	1 skein	branches, wings
✶✶	#443 medium brown	1 skein	branches
··	#819 light baby pink	1 skein	flowers, wings
ZZ	#3689 light mauve	1 skein	wings, shirt, flowers
XX	#3688 medium mauve	1 skein	buds, shirt, wings
SS	#3326 light rose	1 skein	flowers, wings
mm	#3687 mauve	1 skein	buds, wings
NN	#3685 dark mauve	1 skein	bud, wing, shoes
++	#917 magenta	1 skein	wings
₿₿	#553 medium violet	1 skein	wings
JJ	#754 light peach flesh	1 skein	cheek, hand
⋀⋀	#225 very light shell pink	1 skein	face, hand
▭	white	1 skein	hair
▰	#310 black	1 skein	hair
CC	#3371 black-brown	1 skein	branches

Figure 9-2

ing as follows: one piece 11 by 11 inches (28 by 28cm); one piece 9 by 11 inches (23 by 28cm); one piece 6 by 11 inches (15 by 28cm).

14. Fold each piece of broadcloth print in half lengthwise to make pieces 12 by 11 inches (30.5 by 28cm), 9½ by 11 inches (24 by 28cm), and 6½ by 11 inches (16.5 by 28cm), respectively. Press. Put the interfacing inside the appropriate folded broadcloth piece and stitch along the fold to hold the interfacing in place. These are the pockets; the folded edge is the top of the pocket.

15. For the left side of the portfolio, stitch the largest pocket to one of the 13-by-11-inch (33-by-28cm) pieces of solid broadcloth along the edges and bottom; take a ¼-inch (.5cm) seam.

16. For the right side of the portfolio, pin the smallest pocket to the medium pocket matching the edges and bottom of the pocket. Sew two seams, one 5 inches (13cm) from the left edge on the smaller pocket, the other 7 inches (18cm) from the left edge. Pin the two pockets to the remaining piece of solid broadcloth, matching the edges and the bottom. Stitch together around edges and bottom with a ¼-inch seam. Then sew a seam down the middle of the pockets through all three layers.

17. Connect the two broadcloth portfolio sides to the corduroy strip, using a ½-inch (1cm) seam. Press all seams flat.

18. Pin right sides together of inside (broadcloth) and outside (corduroy) of portfolio. Sew a ½-inch seam along the top and bottom—the 22-inch (56cm) sides—leaving edges open and being careful not to catch ribbon ties in these seams. Trim seams and turn right side out. Press flat.

19. Topstitch the center corduroy strip along each edge on the inside of the portfolio through all the layers.

20. Slide the cardboard into each side. The batting should face the outside of the portfolio. If you wrap the cardboard and batting in plastic wrap first, it will slide more easily. Pull out plastic gently when the cardboard is in place.

21. Tuck in the rough edges around the cardboard. Using the ladder stitch (see *Finishing Hints*) and a curved needle, stitch the ends of the portfolio closed. Ribbons are pulled free for tying.

22. To make this portfolio extra special, use the line drawings to have stationery printed on pink or cream paper with envelopes to match. Printers need a clean, black line tracing to do the best job.

Figure 9-6. These drawings can be offset-printed on your personal stationery.

CHAPTER TEN

California Poppy Flower Child Cross-Stitch Framed Picture

The California poppy is a bright, cheerful flower, and in California the fairies must take special care to paint them in the spring. The finished design measures approximately 9 by 14 inches (23 by 35.5cm).

MATERIALS

- #14 Aida cloth, white, 12 by 18 inches (30.5 by 46cm)
- DMC embroidery floss. See Color Chart (Figure 10-2)
- Tapestry needle #24
- Frame and mat board (see *Finishing Hints*)

DIRECTIONS

1. Refer to Figures 10-2A and B. The design measures 207 by 125 threads.
2. Zigzag around the edges of the Aida cloth to prevent unraveling.
3. Starting at the center of the fabric, stitch out toward the edges. Use 2 plies of the embroidery floss to cross-stitch the design.
4. Following dark lines on the graph and using 2 plies of the colors mentioned in the Color Chart for the appropriate areas, do backstitching.
5. Wash. Press gently.
6. Cut mat board and frame the design (see *Finishing Hints*).

Figure 10-1. California Poppy Flower Child—stitched by Karen Benight.

Figure 10-2. California Poppy Flower Child chart.

Code	Color	# of Skeins	Design Part
DMC embroidery floss, 8-meter skeins			
OO	#972 light canary yellow	1 skein	flowers, wings, shirt
NN	#741 medium tangerine	1 skein	flowers, wings
HH	#971 pumpkin	1 skein	flowers, wings, shirt
SS	#947 burnt orange	1 skein	flowers, shirt, backstitching on flowers and wings
NN	#500 darkest blue-green	1 skein	leaf, stem, bud, backstitching on leaves and stems
11	#501 dark blue-green	1 skein	leaf, stem
=	#502 blue-green	1 skein	leaf, stem, bud, wings, backstitching on pants
XX	#503 medium blue-green	1 skein	leaf, stem, bud, wings, belt
ZZ	#504 light blue-green	2 skeins	leaf, stem, wings, shirt, pants
TT	#987 dark forest green	1 skein	leaf
··	#746 pale yellow	1 skein	wings, shirt
CC	#783 gold	1 skein	wings, shirt
☐	#743 medium yellow	1 skein	wings
■	#606 bright orange-red	1 skein	wings, shirt, backstitching on shirt
※※	#946 medium burnt orange	1 skein	wings
MM	#225 pale shell pink	1 skein	face, arms
<<	#950 light flesh	1 skein	face, arms
♭♭	#224 light shell pink	1 skein	face

Code	Color	# of Strands	Design Part
66	#223 medium shell pink	1 skein	face, backstitching on arms, around face
AA	#738 pale tan	1 skein	hair
JJ	#437 light tan	1 skein	hair
33	#435 tan	1 skein	hair
—	#434 light brown	1 skein	hair
✓✓	#433 medium brown	1 skein	hair
	#898 very dark coffee brown	1 skein	backstitching on face

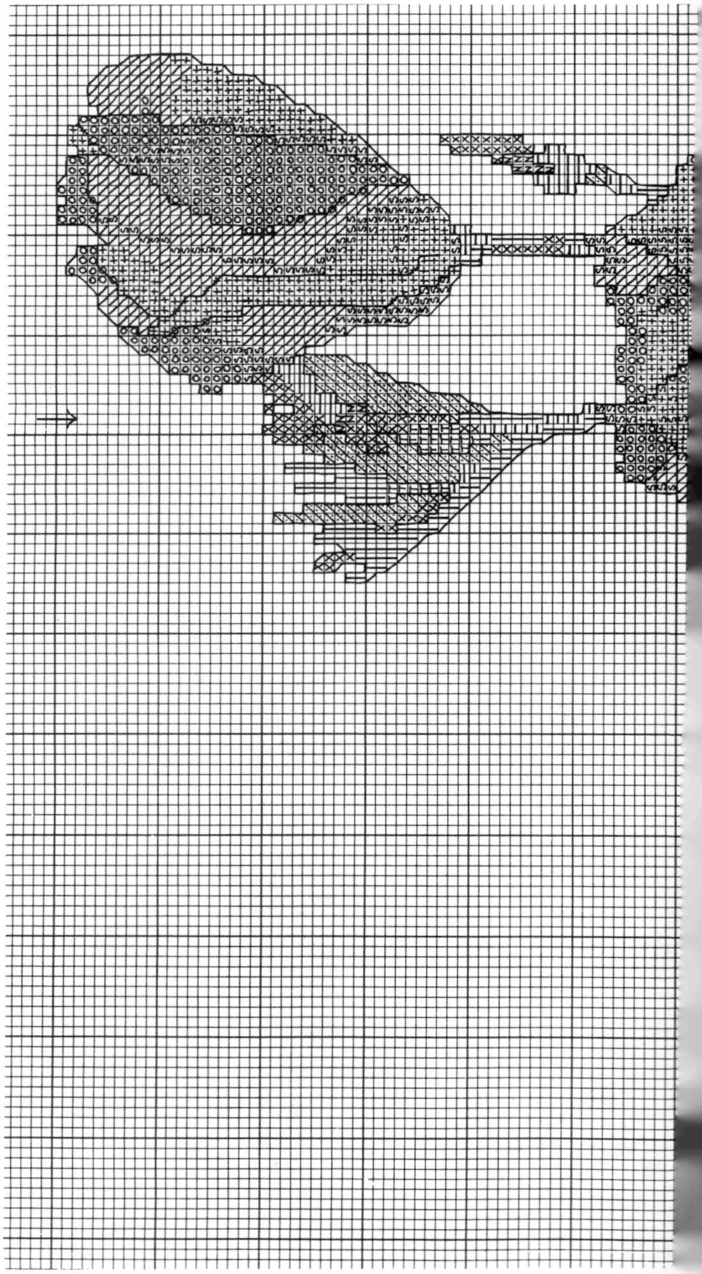

Figure 10-2A

Figure 10-2B

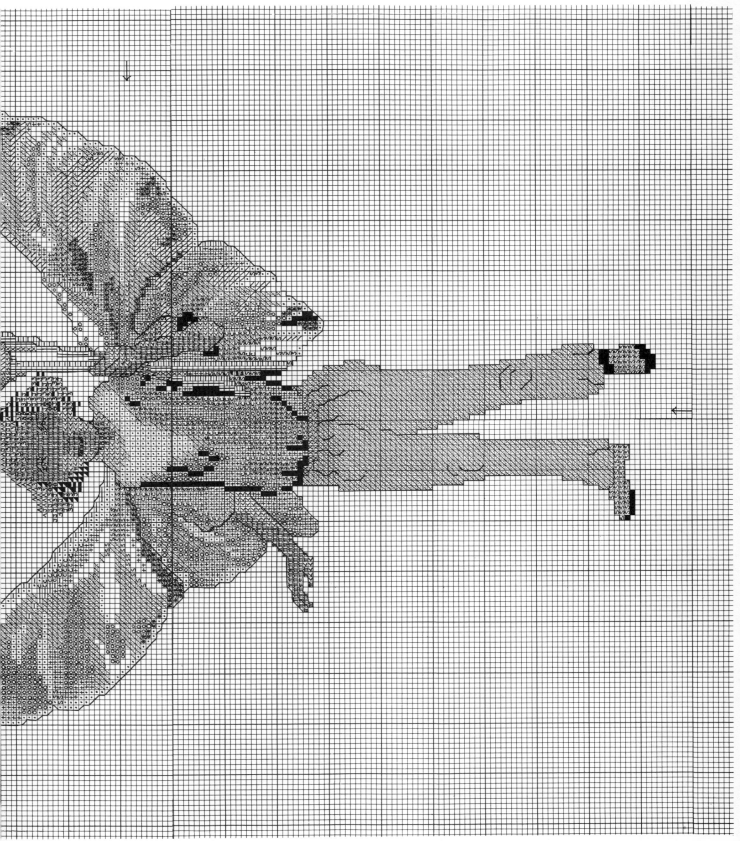

CHAPTER ELEVEN

Rose Baby Cross-Stitch Book Cover

The rose baby was inspired by the old wives' tale that babies were found under a cabbage leaf. Here is a baby found in a rose. The design measures 4½ by 6¼ inches (11.5 by 16cm).

MATERIALS

○ #14 Aida cloth, mint green, 7 by 9 inches (18 by 23cm)
○ DMC embroidery floss, 1 8-meter skeins. See Color Chart (Figure 11-2).
○ Tapestry needle #24
○ Quilted fabric, ½ yard (46cm)
○ Lining fabric, ½ yard (46cm)
○ Ribbon, 1 yard (1m)
○ Eyelet trim, 1 yard (1m)
○ Baby book (for keeping records, sold in most stationery stores)
○ Simplicity Pattern 5296 (optional), or any book cover pattern

DIRECTIONS

1. Refer to Figure 11-2. The design measures 69 by 57 threads.
2. Zigzag around the edges of the Aida cloth to prevent unraveling.
3. Start in the center and work outward toward the edges. Use 3 plies of the embroidery floss to cross-stitch the design.
4. Backstitch with 2 plies of #433 brown embroidery floss when cross-stitching is completed; use dark lines on the graph as a guide.
5. Make a French knot for each eye with 2 plies of #433 brown embroidery floss.

6. Wash. Press gently.
7. Now you are ready to make the book cover. Measure book height and around width of book.
8. Cut quilted fabric as follows: one piece that is book height plus 1 inch (2.5cm) by 2 times the book width plus 1 inch; one piece that is book height plus 1 inch by book width minus 4 inches (10cm); and 2 pieces that are book height plus 1 inch by 4 inches (see Figure 12-3).
9. On largest rectangle draw an oval—4½ by 6¼ inches (11.5 by 16cm)—centered on one side on the back of the fabric. With the right sides together, pin lining fabric to the quilted fabric over oval. Sew around the oval. Cut out center of the oval, trim to ¼ inch and (.5cm) and clip the curves. Turn the lining oval to the back of the quilted fabric. Press.
10. Center the cross-stitch under the oval, pin to the quilted fabric, and sew around the oval on the quilted fabric to hold the cross-stitch in place.
11. Thread the ribbon through the eyelet, pin in place on the cover (see Figure 11-3), and sew down the center of the ribbon to attach to the cover.
12. Hem one side of each 4-inch-wide flap ½ inch (1cm). With right sides together, pin the unhemmed side of each flap to one edge of book cover. Sew a ½-inch (1cm) seam along top and bottom edges of flap.
13. Hem right and left edge of the inside cover (medium rectangle). Pin right side of the inside cover

Figure 11-1. Rose Baby—
stitched by Pam Trask.

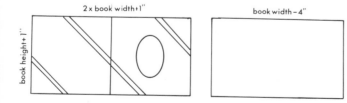

Figure 11-3. Measurements of pattern pieces for book
cover.

centered on the right side of quilted cover and overlapping flaps 1 inch (2.5 cm). Sew along the top and
the bottom with a ½-inch (1cm) seam. Turn the
cover right side out, then turn flaps right side out.
14. Place book cover in the fabric cover.

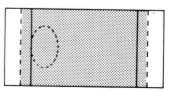

Figure 11-4. How to sew overlapping pieces.

Figure 11-2. Rose Baby chart.

Code	Color	# of Skeins	Design Part
DMC embroidery floss, 8-meter skeins			
⟋⟋	#783 gold	1 skein	hair
· ·	#948 light flesh	1 skein	baby
++	#754 dark flesh	1 skein	baby
OO	#445 pale yellow	1 skein	rose
=	#726 yellow	1 skein	rose
cc	#725 light gold	1 skein	rose
VV	#977 honey	1 skein	rose
☐	#895 dark green	1 skein	leaves
XX	#905 forest green	1 skein	leaves
III	#906 green	1 skein	leaves
	#433 brown	1 skein	backstitching and French knots

CHAPTER TWELVE

Dragon Blackwork Framed Picture

This dragon blackwork is an adaptation of a dragon needlepoint my mother purchased many years ago. Blackwork is a relatively simple technique that utilizes geometric patterns to fill areas. Its dramatic effect is the result of the high contrast of dark thread on a light-colored fabric. The finished dragon measures 6 by 7.5 inches (15cm by 19cm).

Figure 12-1. Blackwork Dragon—stitched by the author.

Figure 12-2. Dragon Blackwork pattern.

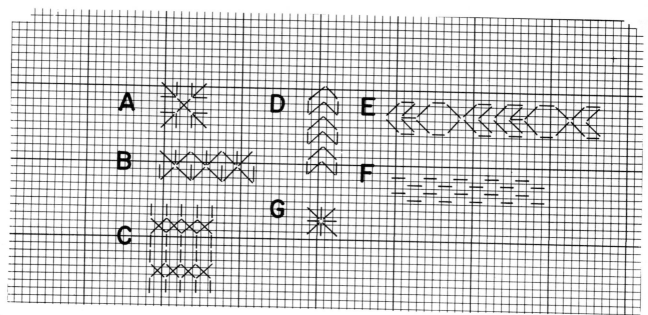

Figure 12-3. Blackwork patterns.

MATERIALS

- #22 Hardanger, gold, 14 by 12 inches (35.5 by 30.5cm)
- DMC embroidery floss, an 8 meter skein of black #310
- DMC Perle cotton (size 8), an 8 meter skein of black #310
- Talon metallic thread, 1 spool of gold
- Tapestry needle #24
- Embroidery needle
- Pressure-fax transfer pen
- Frame approximately 9 by 12 inches (23 by 30.5cm) (see *Finishing Hints*)

DIRECTIONS

1. Zigzag the edges of the fabric to prevent unraveling.

2. Refer to Figure 12-2. Make a dragon transfer from the outline of the dragon. (Be sure to make the transfer of the mirror image, so it will print the positive image.) Center and transfer the design onto the fabric.

3. Using 3 plies of embroidery floss and a tapestry needle, stitch the geometric patterns in their appropriate places. The pattern placement is indicated on the dragon outline by capital letters that correspond to the graphed patterns in Figure 12-3.

4. Using the embroidery needle, outline each of the areas with a strand of Perle cotton. Outline the tail, the eye, and the flame with metallic thread.

5. Make two French knots for the pupil of the eye with Perle cotton (use embroidery needle).

6. Wash. Press gently. Frame (see *Finishing Hints*).

CHAPTER THIRTEEN

Mythical Character Cross-Stitch Alphabet Projects

This alphabet was designed to be used for a wide variety of little projects, such as wooden coasters or a purse. Every letter has its own mythical character. They can be stitched all together on one large panel or used individually for almost any purpose. The wall hanging, coasters, pillow, and purse demonstrate how the use of different fabrics and threads can change the size and texture of the designs for almost any purpose.

THREAD COUNT FOR ALPHABET

	letter height	design height	design width
A	58	79	78
B	60	60	56
C	59	62	59
D	59	61	56
E	56	56	52
F	67	67	73
G	60	60	74
H	77	96	86
I	66	78	69
J	87	87	89
K	67	73	73
L	65	65	51
M	64	64	64
N	58	58	68
O	53	69	59
P	61	61	58
Q	61	61	71
R	58	61	61
S	65	65	62
T	72	76	64
U	55	71	93
V	55	63	50
W	67	67	101
X	63	76	50
Y	68	69	98
Z	55	55	61

MATERIALS FOR ALPHABET PANEL

This alphabet panel would make an excellent wall display for a young child or teenager's room.

○ #14 Fiddler's cloth, 32 by 36 inches (81.5 by 91.5cm)
○ DMC embroidery floss, 8-meter skeins, in the following amounts and colors: 20 skeins of #931 gray-blue, 5 skeins of #3371 black-brown. See also Color Charts for each letter.
○ Tapestry needle #26
○ Fabric for backing (see *Finishing Hints*)
○ Rod (to hang panel on) or frame

DIRECTIONS FOR ALPHABET WALL HANGING

Refer to the appropriate illustration for the letter (see Figures 13-2 through 13-28).
1. Use 2 plies of embroidery floss for cross-stitching and backstitching.
2. Start with the letter A in the upper left-hand corner of the fabric. Leave 1½-inch (4cm) margin of unworked fabric around the edge of the wall hanging.
3. Space all the letters 4 threads apart. Since all the letters are different sizes, use the widest part of the letters to count from. They do not line up in exactly straight lines.

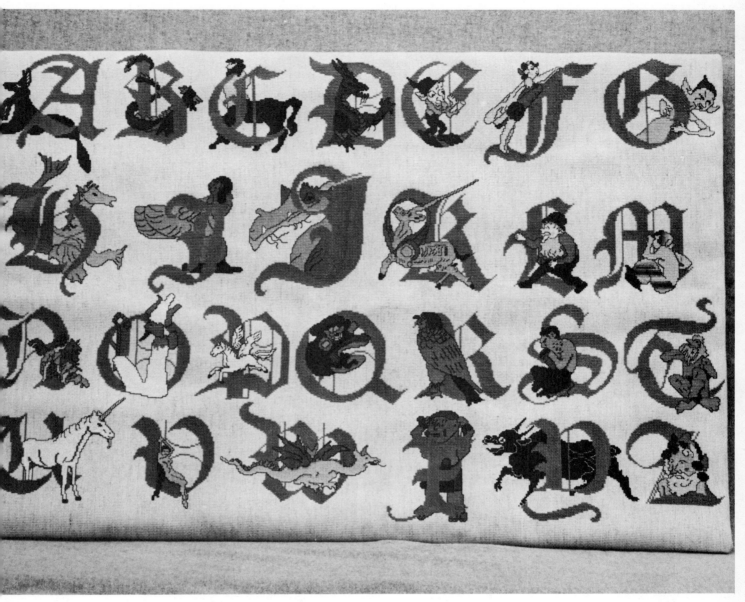

Figure 13-1. Alphabet Panel—stitched by the author.

4. Assemble into a wall hanging or frame (see *Finishing Hints*).

MATERIALS FOR COASTERS

I have picked the four Egyptian characters to make coasters. You could use your initials or the Greek characters, for example, for the same project.

○ #22 Hardanger, natural color, four pieces, each 5 by 5 inches (13 by 13cm)
○ DMC embroidery floss, 1 8-meter skein of each color for Anubis, Isis, Osiris, and Re. For more color variety substitute #921 copper for #931 gray-blue for two coasters and #919 brick and #931 gray-blue in the other two coasters.
○ Wooden coasters, set of four 3-inch (7.5cm) coasters

DIRECTIONS FOR COASTERS

1. Zigzag the edges of the fabric to prevent unraveling.
2. Refer to Figures 13-3 through 13-28. Find the center of the graph and the fabric, and cross-stitch out toward the edges of the design, using 1 ply of embroidery floss.
3. Backstitch around the characters with one ply of #3371 black-brown.
4. Mount the letters in the coasters following the coaster directions. If you wish, glue batting to the cardboard inserts before assembling the coasters.

Figure 13-2. Egyptian Character Coasters—stitched by Karen Benight, Jennifer Robinson, and the author.

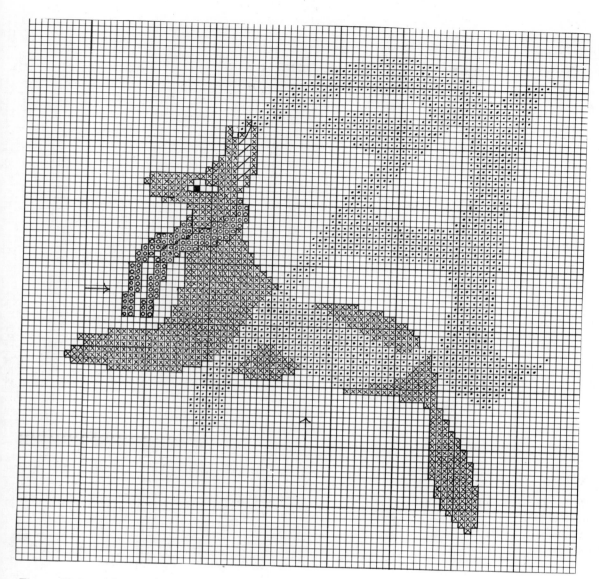

Figure 13-3. Anubis chart.

Code	Color	# of Skeins	Design Part
DMC embroidery floss, 8-meter skeins			
·⊡·	#931 gray-blue	1 skein	letter
⊠⊠	#336 navy blue	1 skein	body
∘∘	#921 copper	1 skein	scarf
▢	white	1 skein	eye
■	#3371 black-brown	1 skein	eye, backstitching

81

Figure 13-4. Basilisk chart.

Code	Color	# of Skeins	Design Part
DMC embroidery floss, 8-meter skeins			
	#931 gray-blue	1 skein	letter
	#606 bright orange-red	1 skein	body
	#970 light pumpkin	1 skein	wings, comb, tail
	#742 light tangerine	1 skein	fins
	#3371 black-brown	1 skein	backstitching

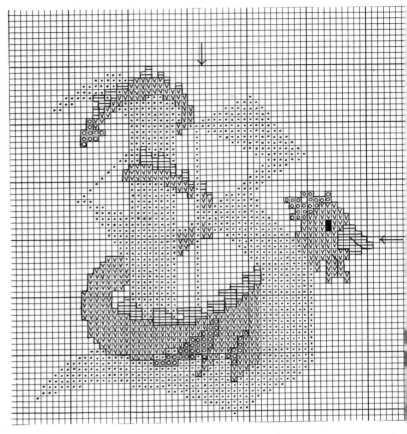

Figure 13-5. Centaur chart.

Code	Color	# of Skeins	Design Part
DMC embroidery floss, 8-meter skeins			
	#931 gray-blue	1 skein	letter
	#945 flesh	1 skein	skin
	#433 medium brown	1 skein	body, tail, hair, beard
	#801 dark coffee brown	1 skein	legs
	#3371 black-brown	1 skein	hooves, eye, backstitching

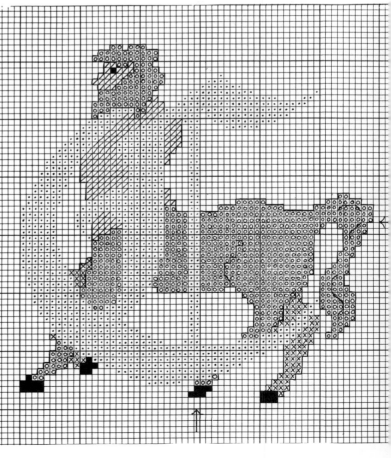

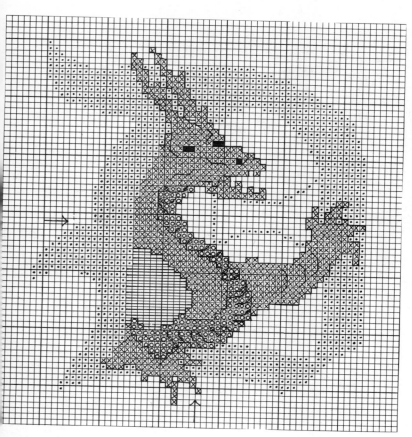

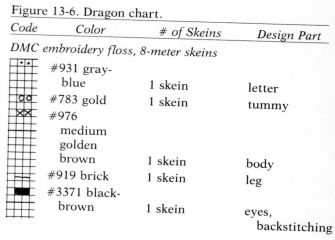

Figure 13-6. Dragon chart.

Code	Color	# of Skeins	Design Part
DMC embroidery floss, 8-meter skeins			
·	#931 gray-blue	1 skein	letter
∞	#783 gold	1 skein	tummy
✕	#976 medium golden brown	1 skein	body
	#919 brick	1 skein	leg
■	#3371 black-brown	1 skein	eyes, backstitching

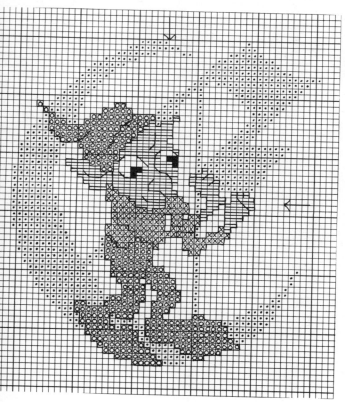

Figure 13-7. Elf chart.

Code	Color	# of Skeins	Design Part
DMC embroidery floss, 8-meter skeins			
·	#931 gray-blue	1 skein	letter
∞	#550 very dark violet	1 skein	pants, hat
✕	#996 medium electric blue	1 skein	shirt
	#818 baby pink	1 skein	face, hands
▭	white	1 skein	eyes
■	#3371 black-brown	1 skein	eyes, backstitching

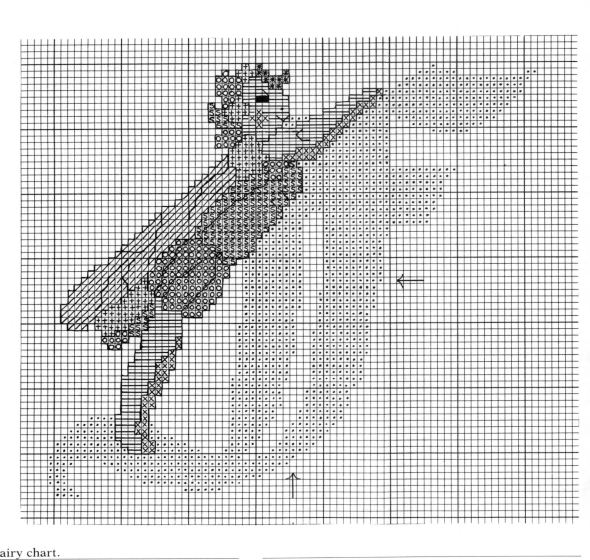

Figure 13-8. Fairy chart.

Code	Color	# of Skeins	Design Part
DMC embroidery floss, 8-meter skeins			
	#931 gray-blue	1 skein	letter
	#818 baby pink	1 skein	face, leg, arm
✗✗	#776 pink	1 skein	cheek, leg, arm
○○	#600 very dark cranberry	1 skein	pants, wreath, wing, sleeve

Code	Color	# of Strands	Design Part
S S	#335 rose	1 skein	shirt, wreath, wing
+ +	#605 pale cranberry	1 skein	sleeve, wing, wreath
✳✳	#781 dark topaz	1 skein	hair
⧄	#211 light lavender	1 skein	wing
■	#3371 black-brown	1 skein	eye, backstitching

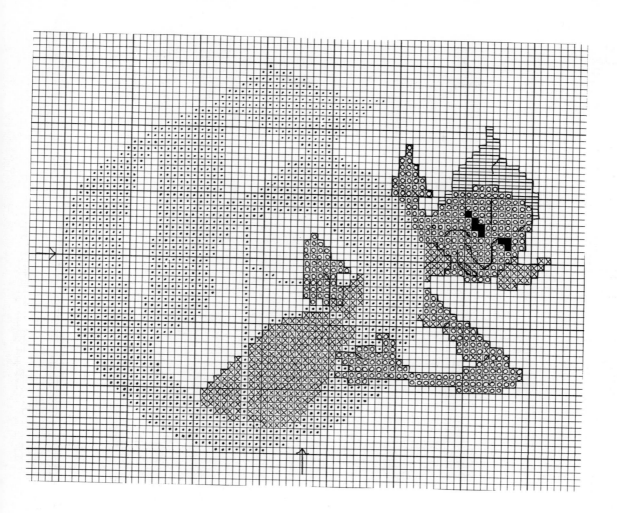

Figure 13-9. Goblin chart.

Code	Color	# of Skeins	Design Part
DMC embroidery floss, 8-meter skeins			
	#931 gray-blue	1 skein	letter
	#754 light peach flesh	1 skein	skin
	#761 light salmon	1 skein	skin
	#943 medium aquamarine	1 skein	hat
	#3371 black-brown	1 skein	eyes, backstitching

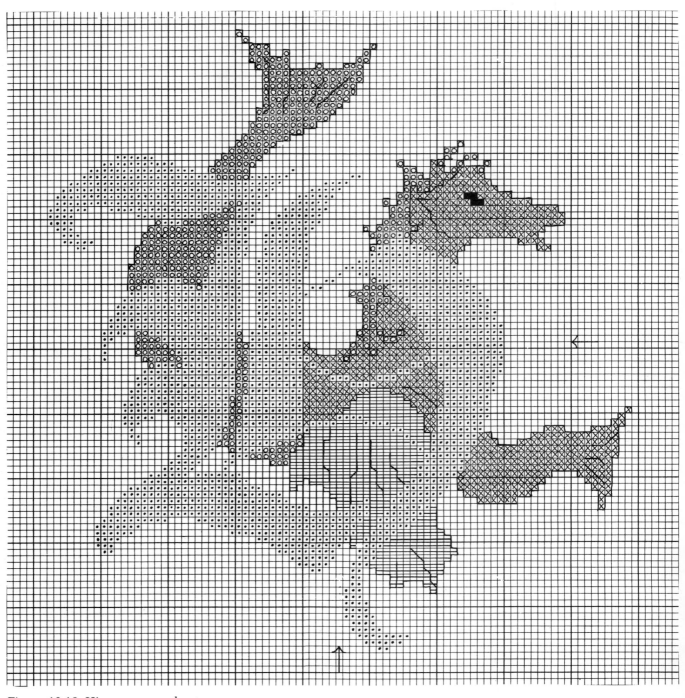

Figure 13-10. Hippocampus chart.

Code	Color	# of Skeins	Design Part
DMC embroidery floss, 8-meter skeins			
⸳⸳	#931 gray-blue	1 skein	letter
oo	#704 lime-green	1 skein	tail, mane
✕✕	#598 light turquoise	1 skein	body

Code	Color	# of Strands	Design Part
	#996 medium electric blue	1 skein	wing
■	#3371 black-brown	1 skein	eye, backstitching

86

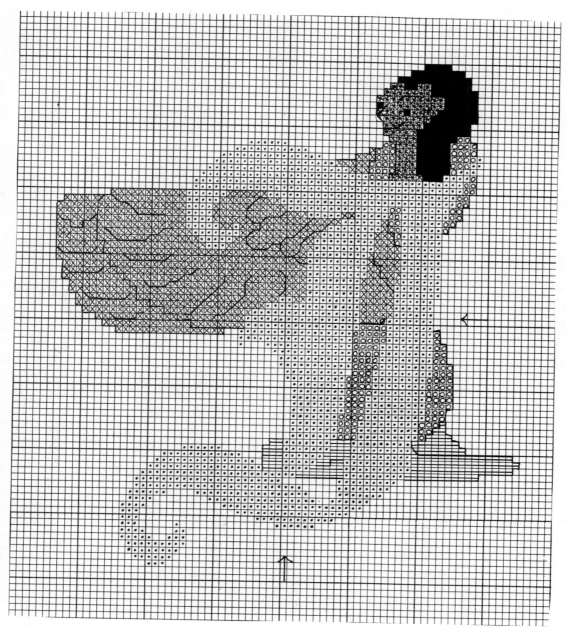

Figure 13-11. Isis chart.

Code	Color	# of Skeins	Design Part
DMC embroidery floss, 8-meter skeins			
··	#931 gray-blue	1 skein	letter
XX	#725 topaz	1 skein	wings
OO	#992 aquamarine	1 skein	dress
=	#991 dark aquamarine	1 skein	dress
✳✳	#922 light copper	1 skein	face
■	#3371 black-brown	1 skein	eye, hair, backstitching

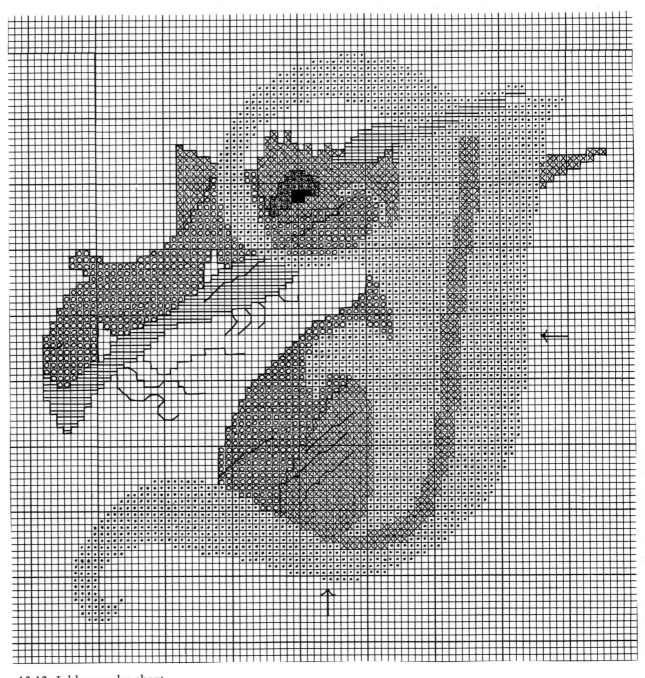

Figure 13-12. Jabberwocky chart.

Code	Color	# of Skeins	Design Part
DMC embroidery floss, 8-meter skeins			
	#931 gray-blue	1 skein	letter
	#552 dark violet	1 skein	body
	#209 dark lavender	1 skein	body, face
	#554 light violet	1 skein	chin, head

Code	Color	# of Skeins	Design Part
	#906 medium parrot green	1 skein	eye
	white	1 skein	teeth
	#3371 black-brown	1 skein	eye, backstitching

88

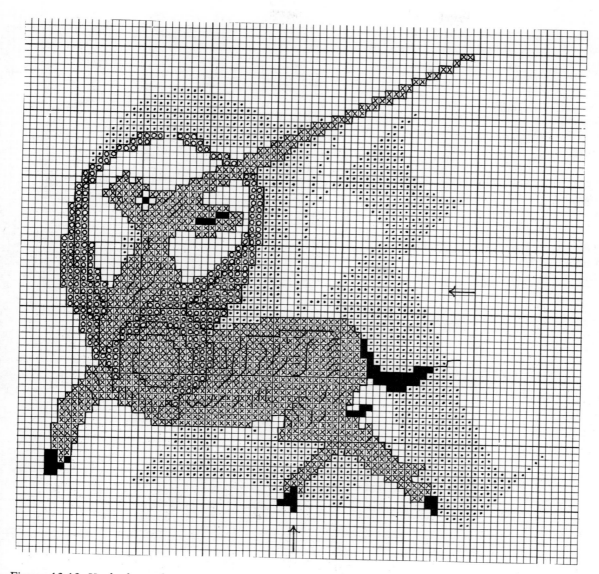

Figure 13-13. Karkadann chart.

Code	Color	# of Skeins	Design Part
DMC embroidery floss, 8-meter skeins			
· ·	#931 gray-blue	1 skein	letter
✕✕	#842 pale beige brown	1 skein	body
○○	#841 light beige brown	1 skein	wings
☐	white	1 skein	eye
■	#3371 black-brown	1 skein	eye, tail, hooves, ear, backstitching

Figure 13-14. Leprechaun chart.

Code	Color	# of Skeins	Design Part
DMC embroidery floss, 8-meter skeins			
	#931 gray-blue	1 skein	letter
	#700 kelly green	1 skein	pants, hat
	#704 lime green	1 skein	shirt
	#3072 gray	1 skein	beard
	#819 baby pink	1 skein	face, hands
	#776 pink	1 skein	cheek
	#783 gold	1 skein	buckle
	#3371 black-brown	1 skein	belt, shoes, backstitching

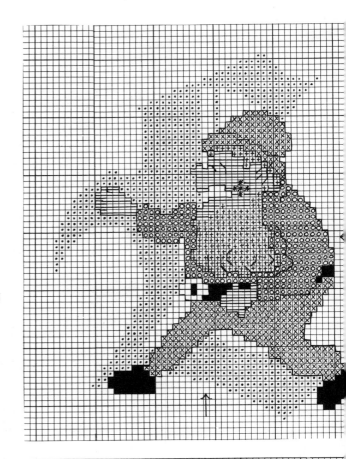

Figure 13-15. Mermaid chart.

Code	Color	# of Skeins	Design Part
DMC embroidery floss, 8-meter skeins			
	#931 gray-blue	1 skein	letter
	#909 very dark emerald green	1 skein	tail fin
	#754 light peach flesh	1 skein	skin
	#760 salmon	1 skein	skin
	#123 variegated green	1 skein	tail, hair
	#3371 black-brown	1 skein	eye, backstitching

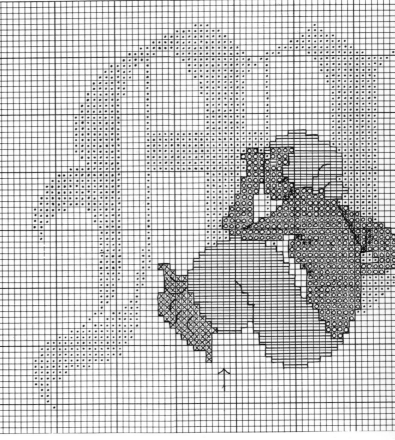

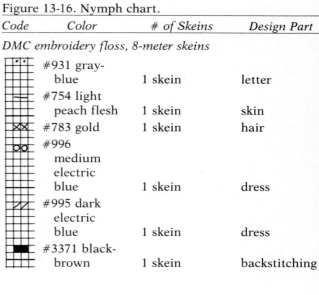

Figure 13-16. Nymph chart.

Code	Color	# of Skeins	Design Part
DMC embroidery floss, 8-meter skeins			
⊡	#931 gray-blue	1 skein	letter
⊟	#754 light peach flesh	1 skein	skin
⊠	#783 gold	1 skein	hair
◎	#996 medium electric blue	1 skein	dress
⊘	#995 dark electric blue	1 skein	dress
■	#3371 black-brown	1 skein	backstitching

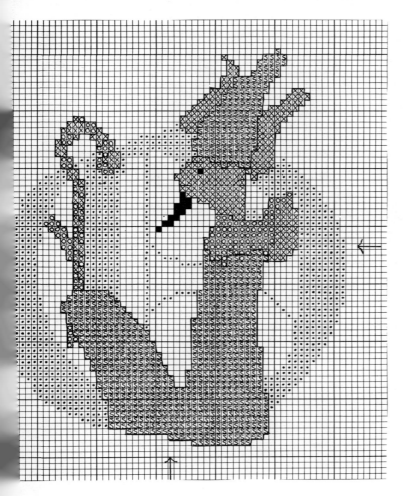

Figure 13-17. Osiris chart.

Code	Color	# of Skeins	Design Part
DMC embroidery floss, 8-meter skeins			
⊡	#931 gray-blue	1 skein	letter
⊠	#992 aquamarine	1 skein	face, hat, staff
◎	#729 medium old gold	1 skein	collar, staff
SS	white	1 skein	clothing
■	#3371 black-brown	1 skein	bread, eye, backstitching

Figure 13-18. Pegasus chart.

Code	Color	# of Skeins	Design Part
DMC embroidery floss, 8-meter skeins			
	#931 gray-blue	1 skein	letter
	white	1 skein	body
	#414 dark steel gray	1 skein	shading
	#3371 black-brown	1 skein	eye, hooves, backstitching

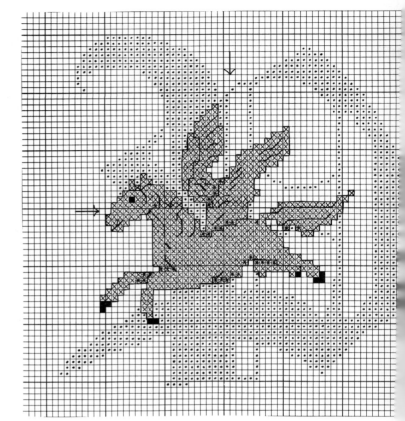

Figure 13-19. Quetzalcoatl chart.

Code	Color	# of Skeins	Design Part
DMC embroidery floss, 8-meter skeins			
	#931 gray-blue	1 skein	letter
	#987 dark forest green	1 skein	head
	#700 kelly green	1 skein	scales
	#704 lime green	1 skein	face
	#797 royal blue	1 skein	lip
	#321 Christmas red	1 skein	tongue
	#444 dark lemon yellow	1 skein	eye, eyebrow
	white	1 skein	eye
	#3371 black-brown	1 skein	eye, backstitching

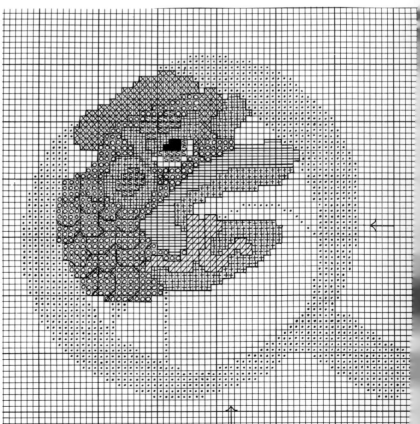

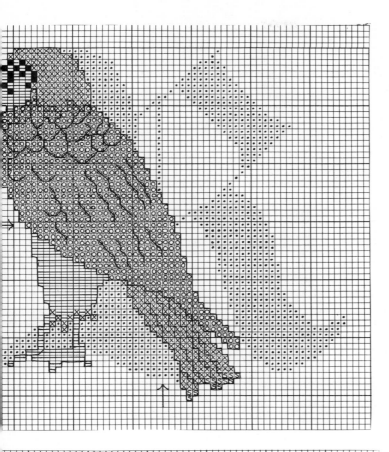

Figure 13-20. Re chart.

Code	Color	# of Skeins	Design Part
DMC embroidery floss, 8-meter skeins			
⊡	#931 gray-blue	1 skein	letter
XX	#991 dark aquamarine	1 skein	feathers
∞	#992 aquamarine	1 skein	feathers
—	#729 medium old gold	1 skein	face, legs
SS	#919 brick	1 skein	tail spots
■	#3371 black-brown	1 skein	backstitching, beak, eye

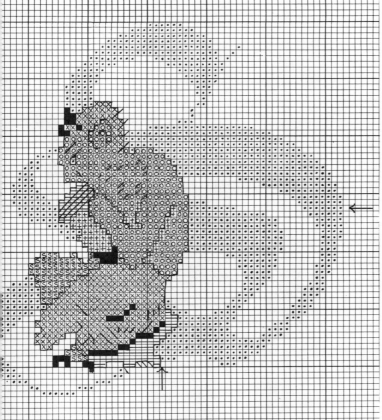

Figure 13-21. Satyr chart.

Code	Color	# of Skeins	Design Part
DMC embroidery floss, 8-meter skeins			
⊡	#931 gray-blue	1 skein	letter
XX	#898 very dark coffee brown	1 skein	leg, hair
SS	#3021 dark gray-brown	1 skein	leg
—	#783 gold	1 skein	leg
∞	#437 light tan	1 skein	skin
++	#435 pale brown	1 skein	skin
■	#3371 black-brown	1 skein	horns, hooves, backstitching

Figure 13-22. Troll chart.

Code	Color	# of Skeins	Design Part
DMC embroidery floss, 8-meter skeins			
⊡	#931 gray-blue	1 skein	letter
◿	#437 light tan	1 skein	face, feet
◉◉	#732 olive green	1 skein	pants
✻✻	#734 light olive green	1 skein	pants
✕✕	#501 dark blue green	1 skein	shirt
⊟	#503 medium blue green	1 skein	shirt
⧄	#928 light gray-green	1 skein	beard
■	#3371 black-brown	1 skein	eye, backstitching

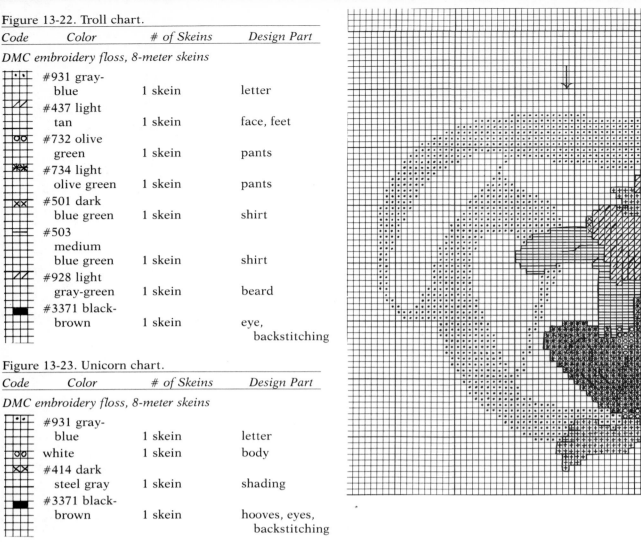

Figure 13-23. Unicorn chart.

Code	Color	# of Skeins	Design Part
DMC embroidery floss, 8-meter skeins			
⊡	#931 gray-blue	1 skein	letter
◉◉	white	1 skein	body
✕✕	#414 dark steel gray	1 skein	shading
■	#3371 black-brown	1 skein	hooves, eyes, backstitching

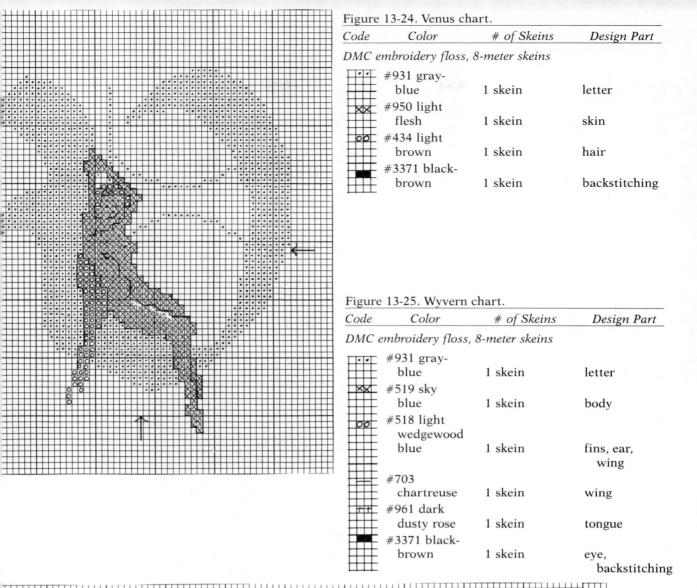

Figure 13-24. Venus chart.

Code	Color	# of Skeins	Design Part
DMC embroidery floss, 8-meter skeins			
· ·	#931 gray-blue	1 skein	letter
✕✕	#950 light flesh	1 skein	skin
○○	#434 light brown	1 skein	hair
■	#3371 black-brown	1 skein	backstitching

Figure 13-25. Wyvern chart.

Code	Color	# of Skeins	Design Part
DMC embroidery floss, 8-meter skeins			
· ·	#931 gray-blue	1 skein	letter
✕✕	#519 sky blue	1 skein	body
○○	#518 light wedgewood blue	1 skein	fins, ear, wing
—	#703 chartreuse	1 skein	wing
╫	#961 dark dusty rose	1 skein	tongue
■	#3371 black-brown	1 skein	eye, backstitching

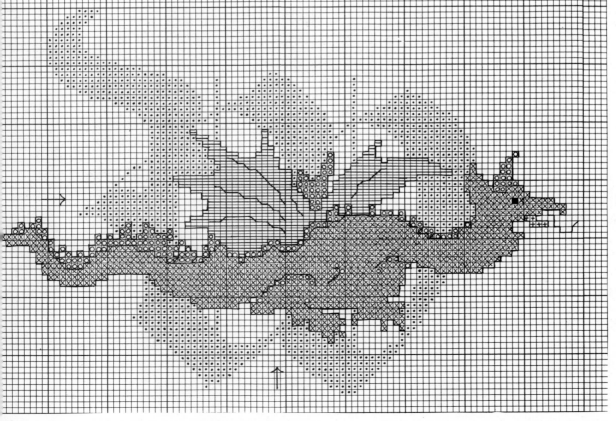

Figure 13-26. Xipe chart.

Code	Color	# of Skeins	Design Part
DMC embroidery floss, 8-meter skeins			
⊡	#931 gray-blue	1 skein	letter
⊠	#783 gold	1 skein	body
∞	#797 royal blue	1 skein	shirt, hat
▤	#321 Christmas red	1 skein	apron
▧	#917 magenta	1 skein	bracelets, skirt
✳	#701 light Christmas green	1 skein	flowers
■	#3371 black-brown	1 skein	backstitching

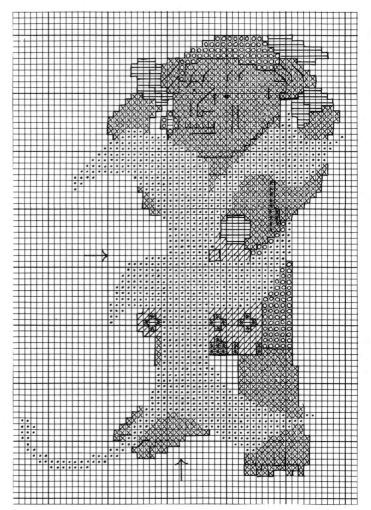

Figure 13-28. Zeus chart.

Code	Color	# of Skeins	Design Part
DMC embroidery floss, 8-meter skeins			
⊡	#931 gray-blue	1 skein	letter
⊠	#950 light flesh	1 skein	skin
∞	#223 medium shell pink	1 skein	shading
▧	#3072 gray	1 skein	beard, hair
✳	#987 dark forest green	1 skein	wreath
▤	#700 kelly green	1 skein	wreath
▦	#704 lime green	1 skein	wreath

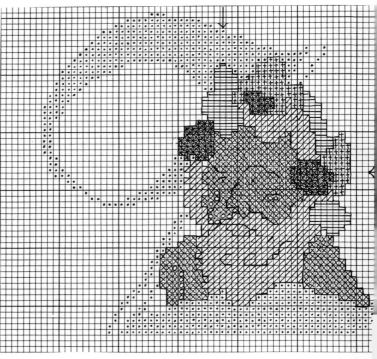

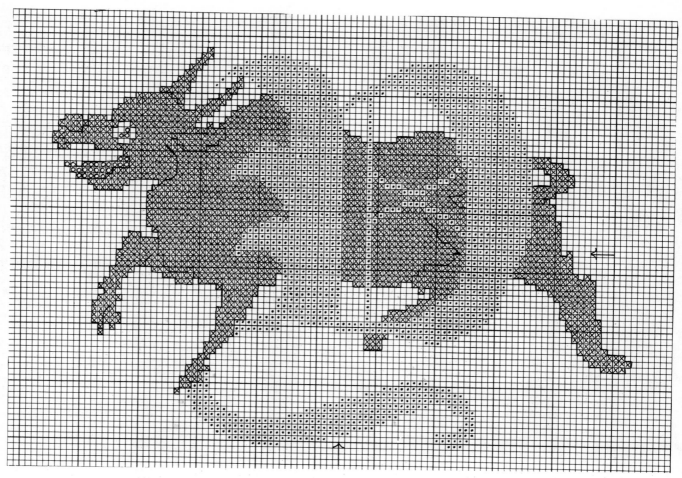

Figure 13-27. Yama chart.

Code	Color	# of Skeins	Design Part
DMC embroidery floss, 8-meter skeins			
	#931 gray-blue	1 skein	letter
	#3371 black-brown	1 skein	body
	#321 Christmas red	1 skein	eye, tongue
	white	1 skein	eye, backstitching

MATERIALS FOR "C" PILLOW

This project was completed to demonstrate that using a large count fabric will enlarge the letter designs to pillow size, and using Smyrna cross-stitch will change the texture. The pillow also shows how the letters can be used alone or if the characters are in front of their letter, they can also be used alone in this manner.

- #7 Wool Java, cream, 19 by 19 inches (48.5 by 48.5cm)
- DMC tapestry wool, 10 8-meter skeins of #7297 navy blue
- Tapestry needle #20
- Fabric for backing and piping (see *Finishing Hints*)

DIRECTIONS FOR "C" PILLOW

1. Zigzag around the edges to prevent the fabric from unraveling.
2. Refer to Figures 13-3 through 13-28. Find the center of the letter and the fabric and stitch toward the edges (see Thread Count Chart). The centaur is *not* stitched. Stitch the entire design in Smyrna cross-stitch (see Figure 13-30) with 1 strand of tapestry yarn.
3. Steam press the design and assemble into a pillow (see *Finishing Hints*).

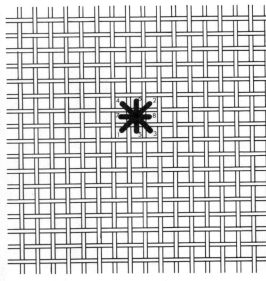

Figure 13-30. Smyrna cross-stitch.

Figure 13-29. "C" pillow—stitched by the author.

MATERIALS FOR MERMAID PURSE

Any of the letters can be made into a purse similar to this one. Since all of the letters are different sizes, some adjustment might be needed in the fabric band dimensions. Calculate the size of the letter you are interested in using by dividing the thread count by the fabric count. For example, 22 threads #22 Hardanger equals 1 inch (2.5cm). Then you can determine how much even-weave fabric you need for the purse and how long the bands for the purse fabric need to be.

○ #22 Hardanger, natural color, 5 by 5 inches (13 by 13cm)
○ DMC embroidery floss, 1 8-meter skein of each color for the mermaid
○ Tapestry needle #26
○ Two cotton prints, ½ yard (45cm) each, (A for outside and B for lining) to coordinate with letter color
○ Woven braid, 1 yard (1m) by 1 inch (2.5cm)
○ Interfacing, ½ yard (46 cm)

DIRECTIONS FOR MERMAID PURSE

1. Refer to Figures 13-15. Cross-stitch the mermaid using 1 ply of embroidery floss.
2. Cut print fabric A as follows: two strips, each 1¾ by 4 inches (4.5 by 10cm); two strips, each 1¾ by 6½ inches (4.5 by 16.5cm); two strips, each 1¾ by 9 inches (4.5 by 23cm); two strips, each 4 by 11½ inches (10 by 29cm); and one piece 11½ by 15¾ inches (29 by 40cm). Cut print B as follows: two strips, each 1¾ by 6½ inches (4.5 by 16.5cm); two strips, each 1¾ by 8¾ inches (4.5 by 22cm); and two pieces, each 11½ by 15¾ inches (29 by 40cm). Cut interfacing into two pieces, each 11½ by 15¾ inches (29 by 40cm).
3. Trim the finished cross-stitch design to 4 by 4 inches (10 by 10cm).
4. With right sides together, at the top and bottom of the cross-stitch, pin the smallest A strips and sew the seam. All seams are ¼ inches (.5cm). Press this and all other seams open. With right sides together, pin the next longer A strips to the sides of the cross-stitch and strips. Sew the seam. Repeat with

Figure 13-31. Mermaid purse
—stitched by the author.

Figure 13-32. Purse measurements.

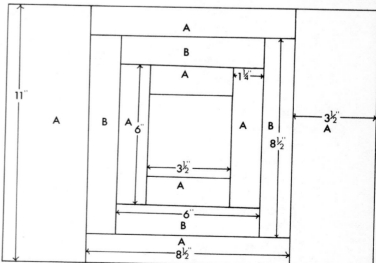

smaller *B* strips around the outside of cross-stitch and strips. Sew the last thin *A* strips to the top and bottom and then the thicker *A* strips to the sides. The front of the purse is assembled.

5. Cut the braid in two pieces. Center and sew one braid piece at each end to the wrong side of the purse front and the other piece to the purse back. Pin the braid out of the way on the right side of the fabric to prevent it from getting caught in other sewing.

6. With right sides together, pin the front and the back of the purse together and sew edges and the bottom. Turn right side out. Press.

7. Baste the interfacing to the wrong side of the two lining pieces.

8. With right sides together, sew the lining pieces together at the edges and the bottom.

9. With right sides together, pin the lining and outside together at the top. Sew around the top, leav-

ing a 3-inch (8cm) space open. Turn the purse right side out and whipstitch the opening closed. **Press.**

99

CHAPTER FOURTEEN

Sea Serpent and Pegasus Cross-Stitch Fabric Boxes

Sea serpents have plagued sailors since man first sailed the seas. This sea serpent design is an adaptation of a Scythian gold brooch. Pegasus, the child of Zeus and Medusa, carried heroes through the air on his back. This flying horse has become a popular motif for anything from stained glass to stickers. The top of the *Sea Serpent box* measures 7½ by 8½ inches (19 by 21.5cm); the top of the *Pegasus box* measures 4½ by 6½ inches (11.5 by 16.5cm).

MATERIALS FOR SEA SERPENT FABRIC BOX

- #14 Aida cloth, light blue, 9 by 9 inches (23 by 23cm)
- DMC embroidery floss, 8-meter skeins. See Color Chart (Figure 14.2)
- Balger blending filament, or any thin metallic thread, as follows: #029 blue-green combined with #909 dark green, #032 pearl combined with all other colors
- Tapestry needle #24
- Corduroy, ¼ yard (23cm)
- Lining fabric, ¼ yard (23cm)
- Button to coordinate
- Trim to coordinate
- Quilt batting, ½ yard (46cm)
- Noncorrugated cardboard, 9 by 27 inches (23 by 68.5cm)
- Cord elastic
- White glue
- Double-sided masking tape
- Curved needle
- Sewing thread

DIRECTIONS FOR SEA SERPENT FABRIC BOX

1. Zigzag around the edges of the Aida cloth to prevent unraveling.
2. Refer to Figure 14-2. Find the center of the fabric and cross-stitch design out toward the edges. Use 2 plies of the embroidery floss and one strand of Balger blending filament to cross-stitch the design.
3. Backstitch the design with 2 plies of #3371 black-brown, following the dark line on the graph.
4. Wash and press gently.
5. Now you are ready to assemble the box. Cut cardboard into hexagons and rectangles as follows: four hexagons, each with 4-inch (10cm) sides; six rectangles, each 4 by 3 inches (10 by 8cm). See Figure 14-3).
6. Glue batting to one side of each of three hexagons and to both sides of all six rectangles. Set aside to dry.
7. Cut a strip of corduroy and lining, each 4½ by 26 inches (11.5 by 66cm). With right sides together, stitch a ⅜-inch (.9cm) seam along both 26-inch (66cm) edges. Turn right side out. Press.
8. Fold strip in half lengthwise and press gently. Unfold strip and sew along the fold line, thus dividing the strip into two 3¾-by-13-inch (9.5-by-33cm)

Figure 14-1. Sea Serpent —stitched by Colleen Fairbairn.

sections. Machine stitch back and forward two times at the beginning and end of the seam to secure stitching.

9. Slide one cardboard-batting rectangle with batting into the strip until it reaches the middle seam. If you wrap the cardboard-batting in plastic wrap it will slide more easily. Gently pull out the plastic when the cardboard is positioned correctly. Sew a seam as close as possible to the other side of the cardboard to hold it in place. Repeat until all the rectangles fill the strip, leaving the ends open. Tuck the unfinished ends inside and, using the ladder stitch (see *Finishing Hints*) and a curved needle, sew the seam to hold cardboard in place.

10. Sew the two ends of the strip together along the outside, using the ladder stitch and a curved (upholstery) needle.

11. Cut one 9-inch (23cm) square out of corduroy and two 9-inch squares out of lining fabric.

12. Put double-sided tape around the edge of one side (the side without batting) of each of the four hexagons.

13. Place one hexagon, batting side down, on the center of one of the 9-inch squares of lining. Gently pull fabric over to the back of the hexagon and stick to the tape. Trim excess fabric. Repeat for another hexagon and lining square. Then tape the cross-stitch design to a third hexagon. Use square of corduroy to cover the hexagon that does not have batting. This is for the bottom of the box.

14. Cut a 3-inch (8cm) piece of cord elastic, fold in half, and glue to the wrong side, of the cross-stitch hexagon at the front. Glue one lining hexagon to the cross-stitch hexagon and one lining hexagon to the corduroy hexagon. Place a weight on these hexagons to ensure a good bond.

15. Using the ladder stitch and a curved needle, sew corduroy bottom to the strip along all the outside edges. Sew the top to the box along one hexagon side on the inside and the outside.

16. Glue or sew trim around the remaining five sides of the top hexagon to hide the joining groove of the top and lining cardboard.

17. Sew button to the front side of the box.

Figure 14-2. Sea Serpent chart.

Code	Color	# of Skeins	Design Part
DMC embroidery floss, 8-meter skeins			
⋈⋈	#909 very dark emerald green	1 skein	fins and tail
··	#704 lime green	1 skein	body
∞	#369 pale pistachio green	1 skein	tummy
ss	#943 medium aquamarine	1 skein	wing
⊓⊓	#598 light turquoise	1 skein	wing
++	#913 medium sea green	1 skein	wing
■	#3371 black-brown	1 skein	eye, backstitching

Figure 14-3. Cardboard measurements.

cut 4

4"

cut 6

3"

4"

102

Figure 14-4. Pegasus—stitched by Denise
Charlesworth.

MATERIALS FOR PEGASUS FABRIC BOX

- #22 Hardanger, royal blue, 7 by 7 inches (18 by 18cm)
- DMC embroidery floss. See Color Chart (Figure 14-5)
- Tapestry needle #26
- Simplicity Pattern #5296 or any commercial fabric box pattern
- Blue print fabric, 1/4 yard (23cm)
- Lining fabric, 1/4 yard (23cm)
- Trim, 3/4 yard (69cm)
- Ribbon, 1/2 yard (46cm)
- Button
- Noncorrugated cardboard
- Quilt batting
- Curved needle
- White glue

DIRECTIONS FOR PEGASUS FABRIC BOX

1. Zigzag around edges of Hardanger to prevent unraveling.
2. Refer to Figure 14-5. Find the center of the fabric and graph and stitch out toward edges, using 1 ply of embroidery floss.
3. Wash and press gently.
4. Refer to Figure 14-6. Cut cardboard into four elongated hexagons 4 3/8 by 2 3/8 by 2 1/4 inches (10.5 by 6 by 5.5cm), two rectangles 4 3/8 by 3 inches (10.5 by 7.5cm), two rectangles 2 3/8 by 3 inches (6 by 7.5cm)

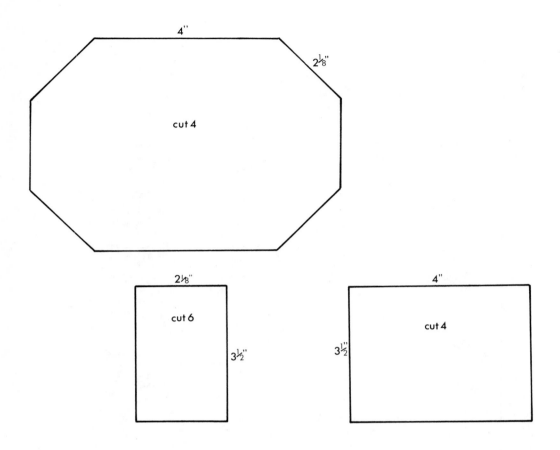

Figure 14-6. Cardboard measurements.

5. Cut fabric as follows: one piece blue fabric, 19 by 3½ inches (48.5 by 9cm), for side; one piece lining fabric, 19 by 3½ inches (48.5 by 9cm), for side; one piece blue fabric, 6½ by 8 inches (16.5 by 20.5cm), for bottom; two pieces lining, 6½ by 8 inches (16.5 by 20.5cm), for top and bottom; two pieces blue fabric, 3 by 6½ inches (7.5 by 16.5cm), for top.

6. Assemble top fabric by topstitching ribbon the sides of cross-stitch design so that it is 4³/₈ (11cm) inches wide. Stitch one piece of blue fabric, 3 by 6½ inches, to either side of the cross-stitch by topstitching the ribbon to them. See photograph for placement.

7. Following the same basic steps as the *Sea Serpent Box*, assemble the *Pegasus Box*. If you are using the commercial fabric box pattern, follow their pattern sizes and assembling directions.

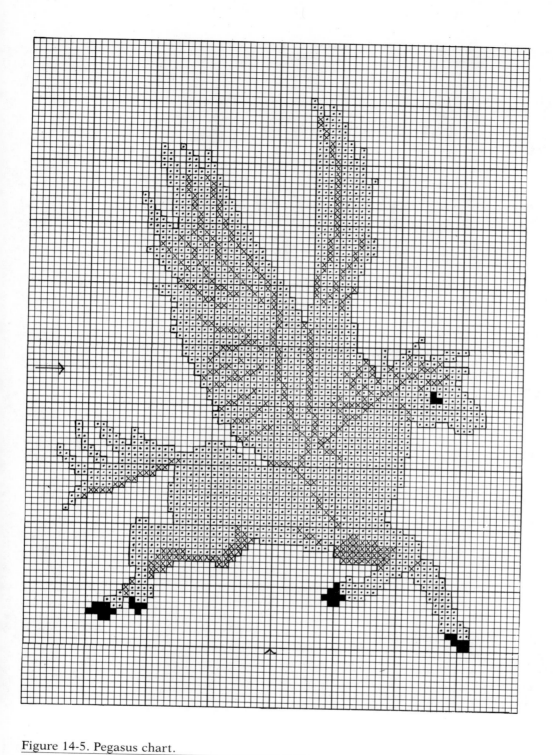

Figure 14-5. Pegasus chart.

Code	Color	# of Skeins	Design Part
DMC embroidery floss, 8-meter skeins			
	white	1 skein	body
	#310 black	1 skein	hooves
	#318 light steel gray	1 skein	body

CHAPTER FIFTEEN

Heracles and Achelous Cross-Stitch Pillow

This cross-stitch pillow was inspired by a Greek vase depicting Heracles and the river god Achelous. Dolphins, also featured on the same vase, are stitched on Aida cloth for the boxing band. The pillow is a 14-inch (35.5cm) circle.

MATERIALS

- #14 Aida cloth, beige: one piece 18 by 18 inches (46 by 46cm) and one piece 46 by 3½ inches (117 by 9cm)
- DMC embroidery floss. See Color Chart (Figure 15-2)
- Tapestry needle #26
- Fabric for backing (see *Finishing Hints*)
- Braid trim—Perle cotton #920 rust (see *Finishing Hints*)

DIRECTIONS

1. Refer to Figures 15-2A and B. The design measures 196 by 196 threads.
2. Zigzag the edges to prevent unraveling.
3. Starting at the center of the chart and the fabric pillow, top, start stitching the scale lines with #437 beige. Fill in the #310 black floss as the scales are done. Use 3 plies of embroidery floss for the entire design.
4. When the design is entirely stitched, backstitch the faces and hair with 2 plies of beige floss.
5. Starting at one end of the Aida strip, center the dolphins on the strip (see Figures 15-3 and 15-4) and complete cross-stitching the dolphins along the strip with 3 plies.
6. Backstitch the dolphins with 2 plies of white embroidery floss.
7. Wash and gently press.
8. Assemble into a round box-edge pillow, following the basic instructions (see *Finishing Hints*) for finishing a box-edge pillow. Sew the Perle cotton braid around the edges of the boxing band after the pillow is assembled.

Figure 15-1. Heracles and Achelous—stitched by Jennifer Robinson.

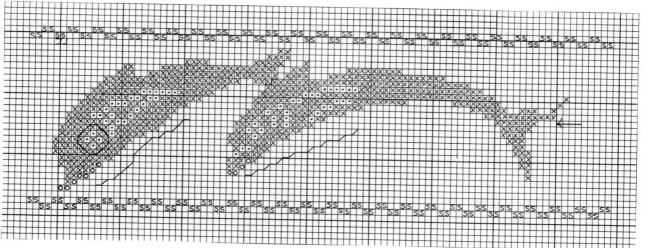

Figure 15-3. Boxing band character chart.

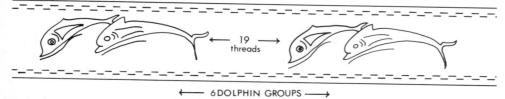

Figure 15-4. Dolphin placement on the boxing band.

Figure 15-2. A Hercules and Achelous chart.

Code	Color	# of Skeins	Design Part
DMC embroidery floss, 8-meter skeins			
⧄	white	1 skein	throughout
✕✕	#310 black	8 skeins	throughout
⦁⦁	#437 beige	3 skeins	throughout
ss	#920 rust	2 skeins	throughout

Figure 15-2A

109   Figure 15-2B

CHAPTER SIXTEEN

Mythical Beast Appliqué Quilt

After attending a quilt show, my fingers were itching to try to appliqué a dragon. I was so pleased with the result, I decided to make a companion design. The next thing I knew, I had a whole quilt of blocks. My *Mythical Beast Quilt* contains nine fantastic creatures, and it measures 80 by 84 inches (203 by 213.5cm).

MATERIALS

- Cotton or cotton/polyester blend broadcloth 44/45-inch (112cm) width, in the following amounts and colors: 5½ yards (5m) of off-white, 1 yard (.9m) of red print, 1 yard (.9m) of gold, 1 yard (.9m) of blue-green, 4 yards (3.5m) of berry, 1 yard (.9m) of blue-green print, 1 yard (.9m) of purple print, and 5 yards (4.5m) of purple
- Batting (traditional weight), 80 by 84 inches (203 by 213.5cm)
- Tracing paper
- Quilting needle
- Quilting thread, 1 spool of off-white and berry
- Black marker
- Quilting pencil, 1 each in white and blue
- Commercial quilting templates—clamshell and double shell (optional)
- Cardboard, ruler, and compass to make templates
- Sewing thread in red, gold, purple, and blue-green

DIRECTIONS

1. Wash to preshrink all fabrics before starting.
2. To enlarge designs for the quilt, make a grid with ½-inch (1cm) squares on tracing paper and trace pattern from the book.

3. Make a grid of 1-inch (2.5cm) squares on another piece of tracing paper. Square by square draw the lines in the 1-inch squares that are in the corresponding ½-inch squares. This should make the design large enough to fill most of the quilt block.
4. For easier tracing, draw over the enlarged drawing with a black marking pen, and tape the drawing up on a window.
5. Cut nine off-white fabric blocks, each 22 by 22 inches (56 by 56cm).
6. Tape the fabric over your tracing paper on the window and use the blue quilting pencil to trace a beast design outline onto each fabric block. Be sure to center design on fabric.
7. To make patterns for appliqué shapes, trace each section of the animal by taping the appropriate color fabric over drawing taped to the window. The capital letters represent the color fabric to use. The lowercase letters indicate which sections can be cut in one piece even though other shapes overlap the piece to be cut. The patterns can be simplified by rounding sharp points and eliminating sharp indentations.
8. Draw a ¼-inch (.5cm) border around each shape, and cut out around this line.
9. Clip curves and points that will be turned under. Do *not* clip or fold under edges that will have other pieces appliquéd over them.

Figure 16-1. Mythical Beast Quilt—stitched by the author.

Figure 16-2. Trace around the outside of the drawing
and transfer the design to the quilt block.

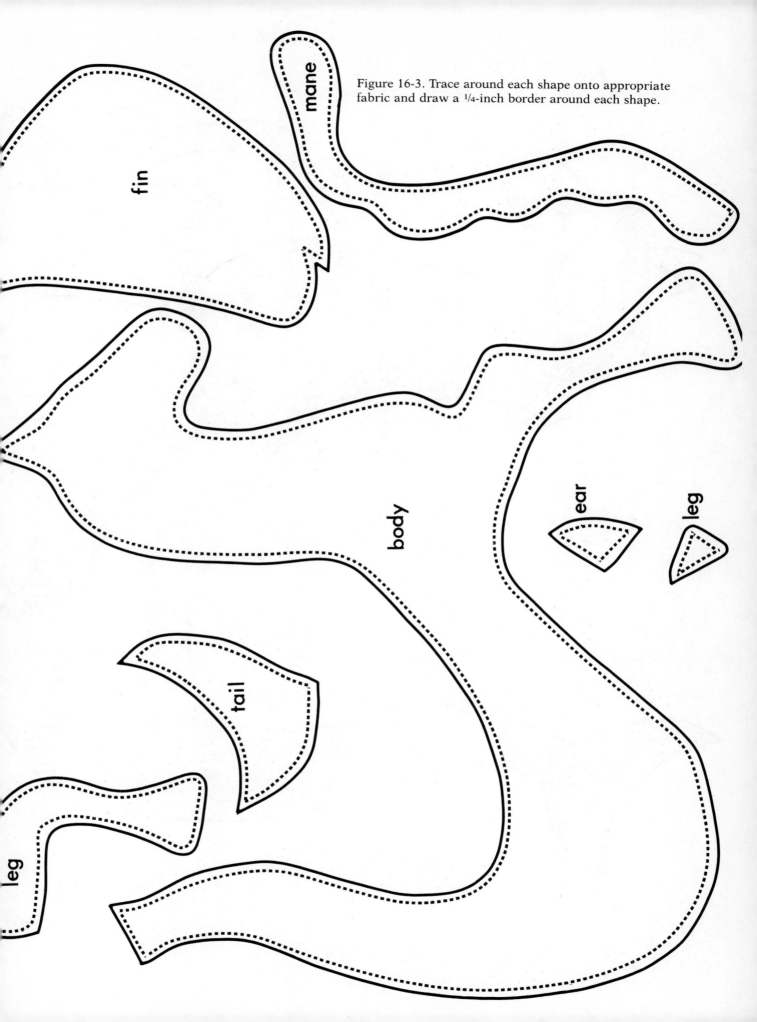

Figure 16-3. Trace around each shape onto appropriate fabric and draw a ¼-inch border around each shape.

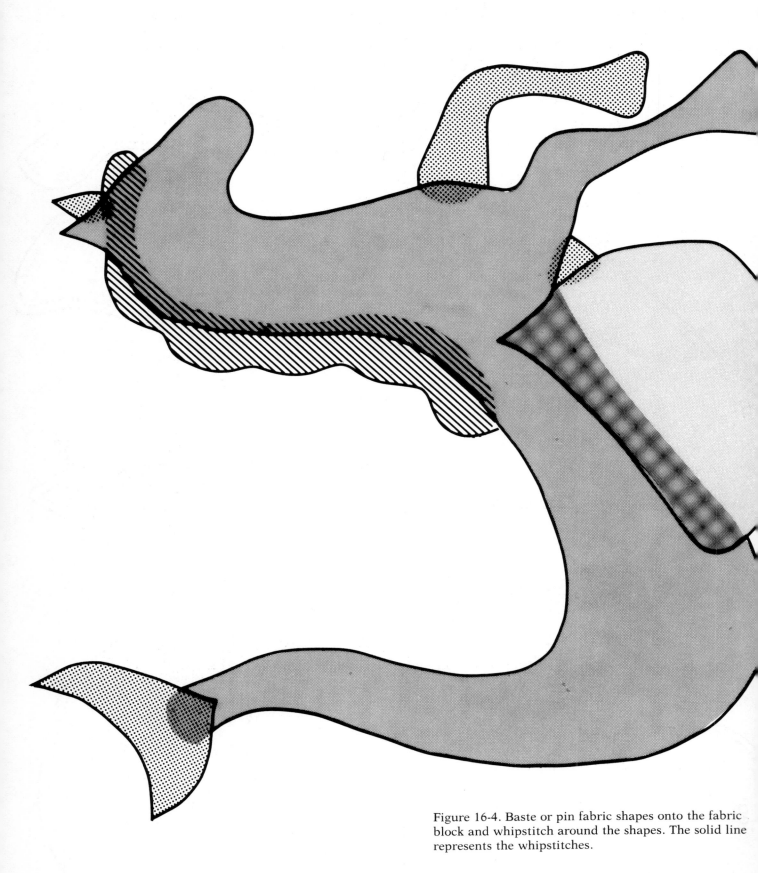

Figure 16-4. Baste or pin fabric shapes onto the fabric block and whipstitch around the shapes. The solid line represents the whipstitches.

114

10. Fold under ¼ inch (.5cm) on the edges that are not overlapped by other shapes. Press down. I have found that basting the hem first made it easier for me to stitch to the fabric block later.

11. Baste or pin the shapes onto the fabric block to hold them in place.

12. Place the fabric block on a hoop (optional) and whipstitch around each shape. Use sewing thread that is the same color as the fabric being whipstitched to the block.

13. Remove all basting thread.

14. Wash the completed quilt square to remove pencil marks. Gently press when almost dry.

15. From berry fabric cut strips for quilt block borders as follows: six strips, each 5 by 22 inches (13 by 56cm); four strips, each 5 by 70 inches (13 by 178cm); and two strips, each 9 by 82 inches (23 by 208cm).

16. Refer to Figure 16-23. Sew quilt blocks to the 5-by-22-inch strips, allowing ½-inch (1cm) seam. Then sew on the 5-by-70-inch strips to the quilt blocks. Sew the 9-by-82-inch strips to the top and bottom of the quilt blocks. Press all seams flat.

17. See Figures 16-24 through 16-26. Cut out templates for cloud, mountain, and wave from cardboard. If commercial clamshell and double shell templates are not available, make templates out of cardboard (See Figures 16-27 and 16-28).

18. Trace appropriate quilting lines around templates on quilt blocks and strips, using quilting pencils (use white on dark colors; blue on light). The cloud pattern is for the dragon, Pegasus, phoenix, and griffin blocks; the wave pattern is for the sea serpent and hippocampus; the mountain pattern is for chimera, unicorn, and basilisk; the clamshell pattern is for the vertical berry strips; the rainbow pattern is for the top and bottom; the wave pattern is for the smaller horizontal berry strips (see photographs).

19. Cut purple fabric into two pieces, each 41 by 84 inches (104 by 213.5cm). Sew these two pieces together along the 84-inch edge, allowing a ½-inch (1cm) seam. The seam goes down the center of the quilt back.

20. Sandwich the batting between the quilt top and quilt back. The quilt top should be 2 inches (5cm) larger on all sides. Baste the three layers together, stitching out from the center of the quilt.

21. Place quilt on a frame or hoop. Using red quilting thread, quilt around appliqué shapes, along quilting lines on animals, around squares, and on patterns on berry strips. Use white quilting thread to quilt waves, clouds, and mountains. Start at the center of the quilt and work out toward the edges.

22. Turn berry fabric under ½ inch (1cm) at the edges of the quilt. Press gently. Turn the berry fabric under toward the purple back. Stitch this hem down with whipstitches to the quilt back.

Figure 16-5. Hippocampus.

Figure 16-6. Unicorn.

Figure 16-7. Basilisk.

Figure 16-8. Sea Serpent.

Figure 16-9. Dragon.

Figure 16-10. Phoenix.

Figure 16-11. Chimera.

Figure 16-12. Pegasus.

Figure 16-13. Griffin.

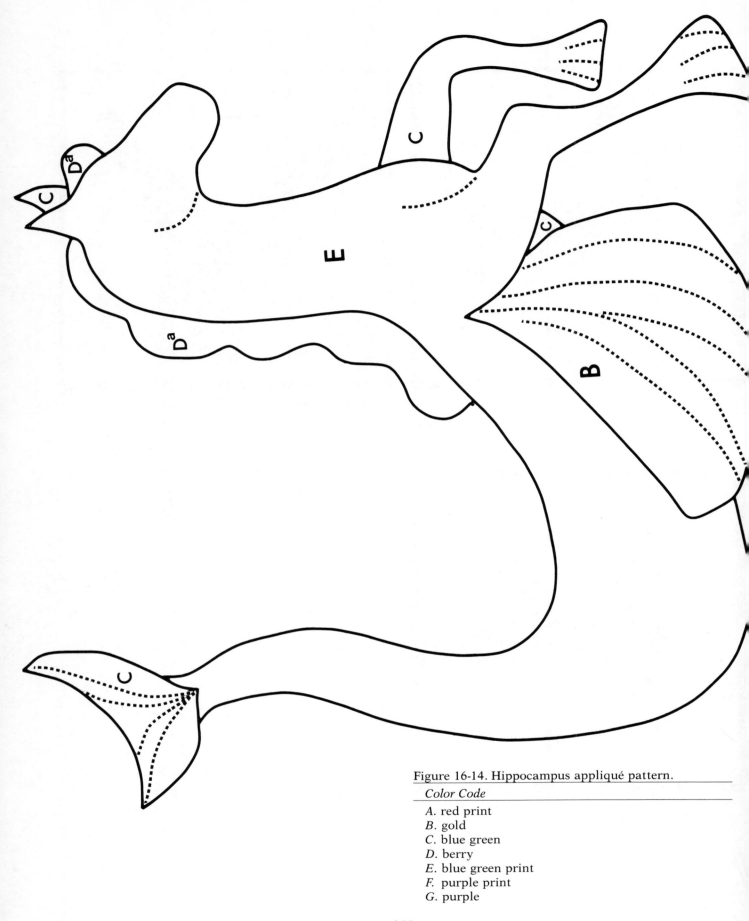

Figure 16-14. Hippocampus appliqué pattern.

Color Code

A. red print
B. gold
C. blue green
D. berry
E. blue green print
F. purple print
G. purple

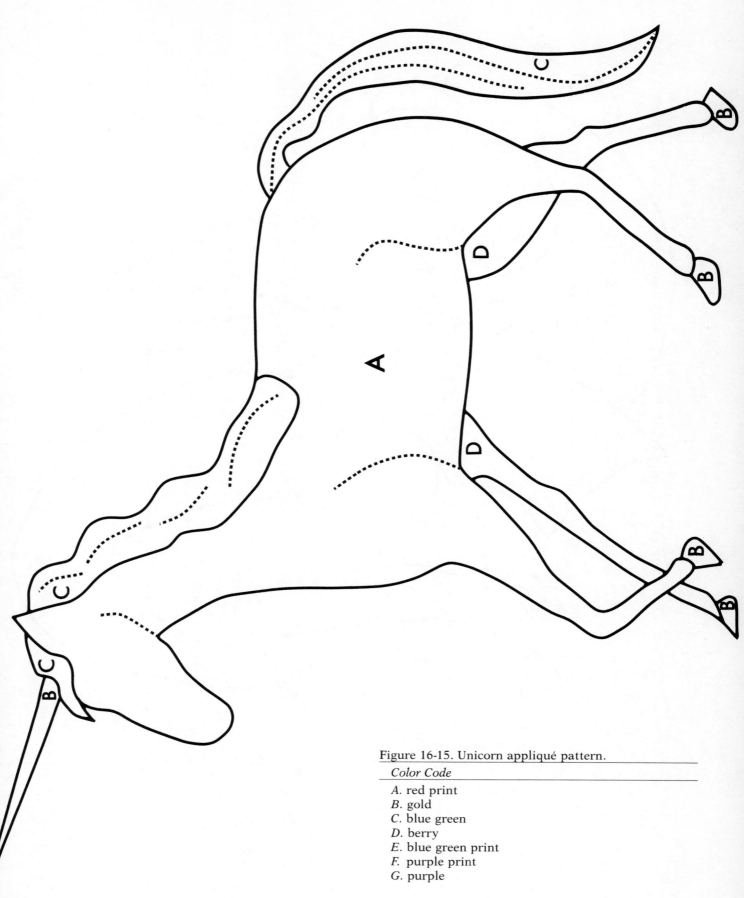

Figure 16-15. Unicorn appliqué pattern.

Color Code

A. red print
B. gold
C. blue green
D. berry
E. blue green print
F. purple print
G. purple

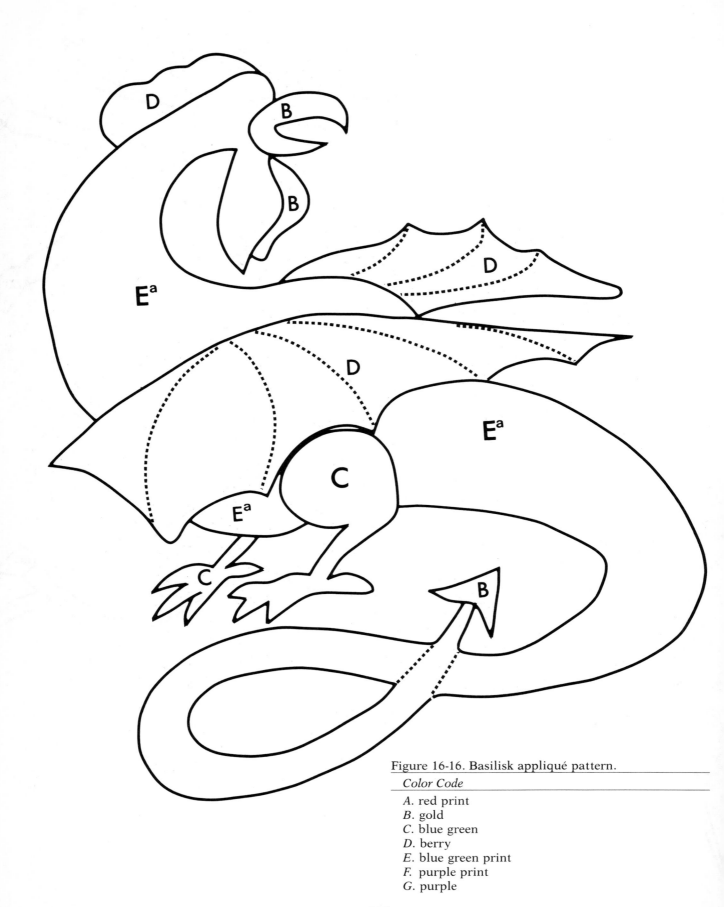

Figure 16-16. Basilisk appliqué pattern.

Color Code

A. red print
B. gold
C. blue green
D. berry
E. blue green print
F. purple print
G. purple

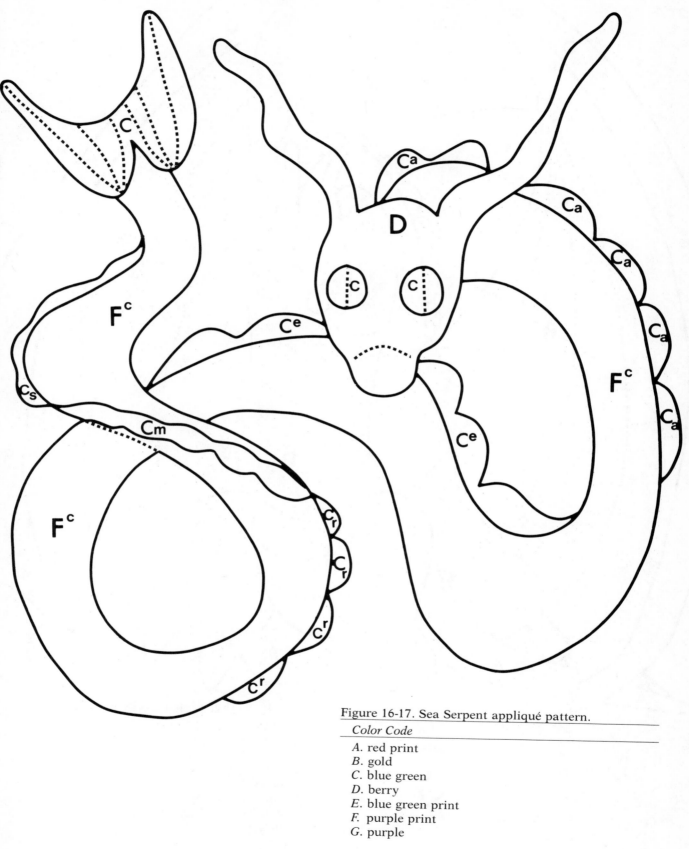

Figure 16-17. Sea Serpent appliqué pattern.

Color Code

A. red print
B. gold
C. blue green
D. berry
E. blue green print
F. purple print
G. purple

Figure 16-18. Dragon appliqué pattern.

Color Code

A. red print
B. gold
C. blue green
D. berry
E. blue green print
F. purple print
G. purple

Figure 16-19. Phoenix appliqué pattern.

Color Code

A. red print
B. gold
C. blue green
D. berry
E. blue green print
F. purple print
G. purple

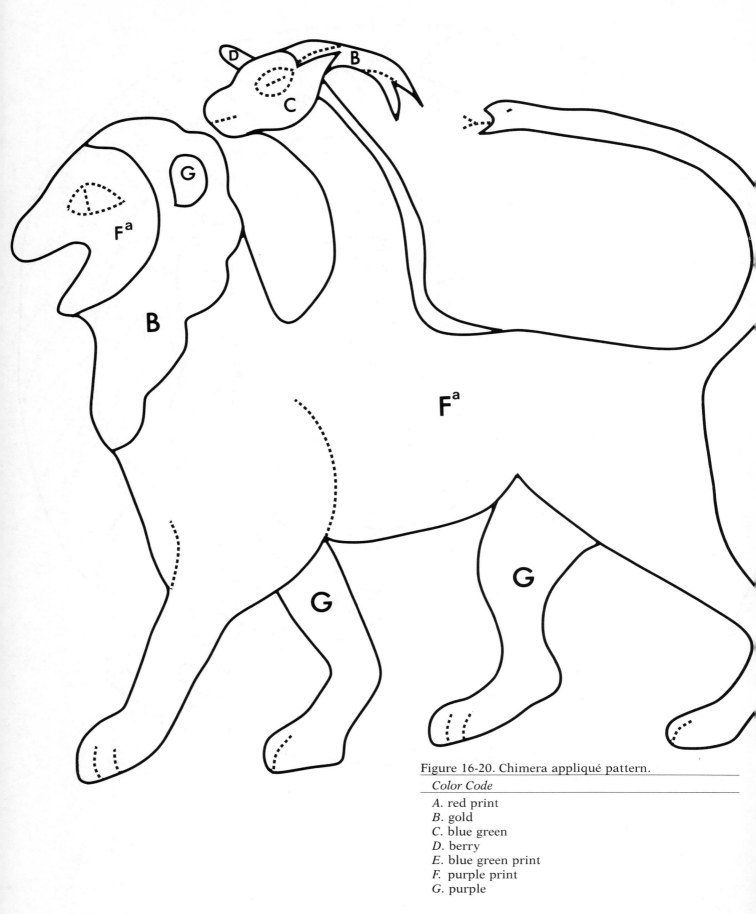

Figure 16-20. Chimera appliqué pattern.

Color Code

A. red print
B. gold
C. blue green
D. berry
E. blue green print
F. purple print
G. purple

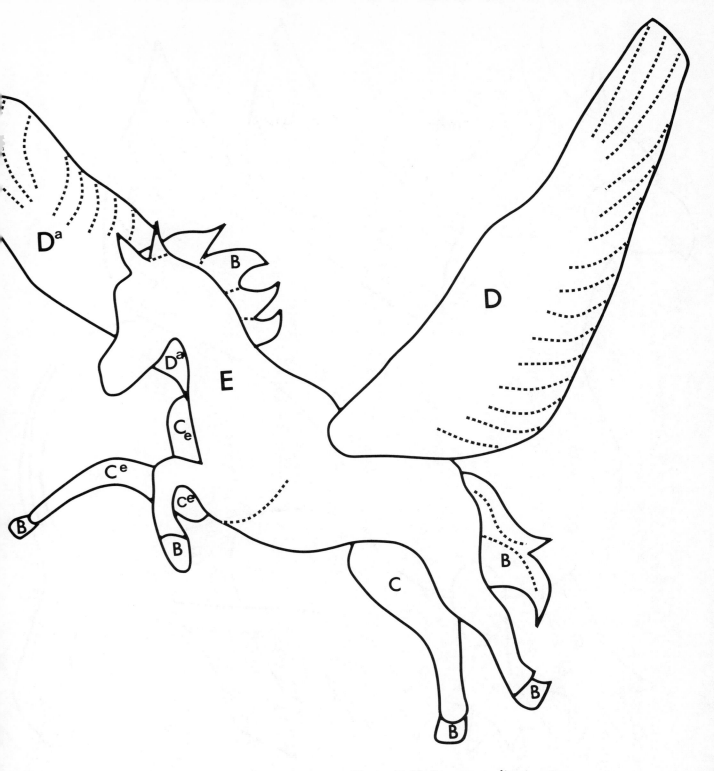

Figure 16-21. Pegasus appliqué pattern.

Color Code

A. red print
B. gold
C. blue green
D. berry
E. blue green print
F. purple print
G. purple

Figure 16-22. Griffin appliqué pattern.

Color Code

A. red print
B. gold
C. blue green
D. berry
E. blue green print
F. purple print
G. purple

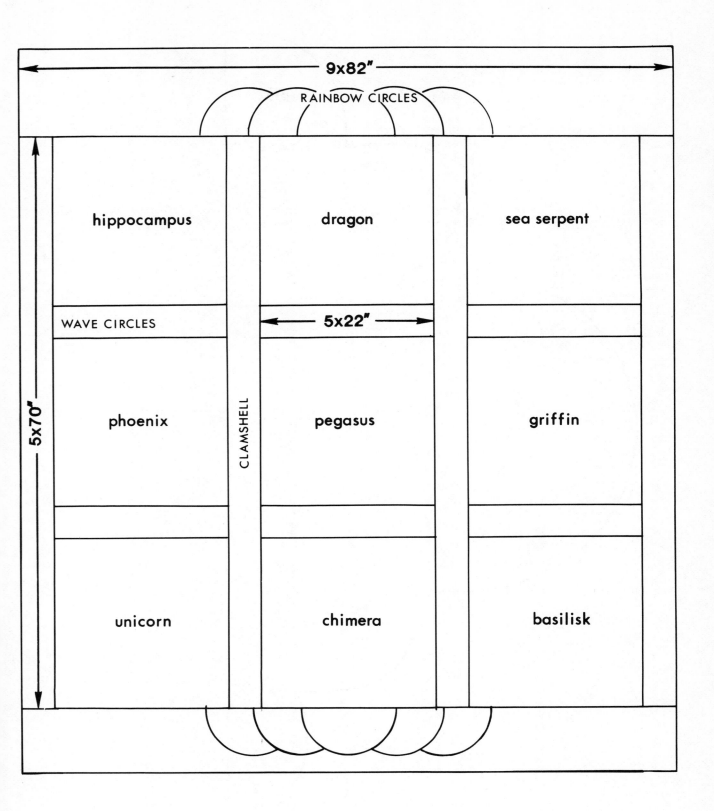

Figure 16-23. Assembled quilt top with quilt design positions.

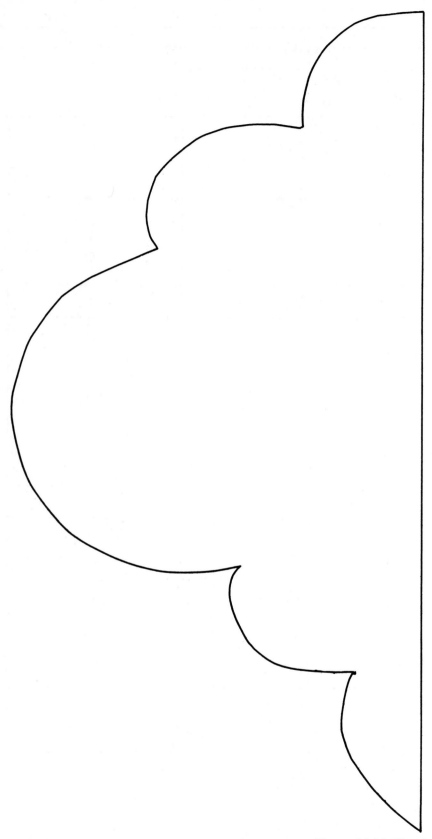

Figure 16-24. Cloud quilt pattern (used for Dragon, Pegasus, Phoenix, Griffin).

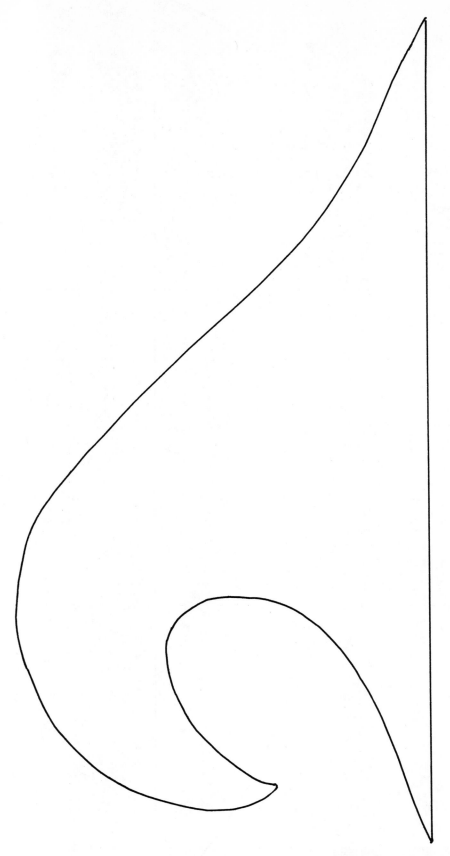

Figure 16-25. Wave quilt pattern (used for Sea Serpent, Hippocampos).

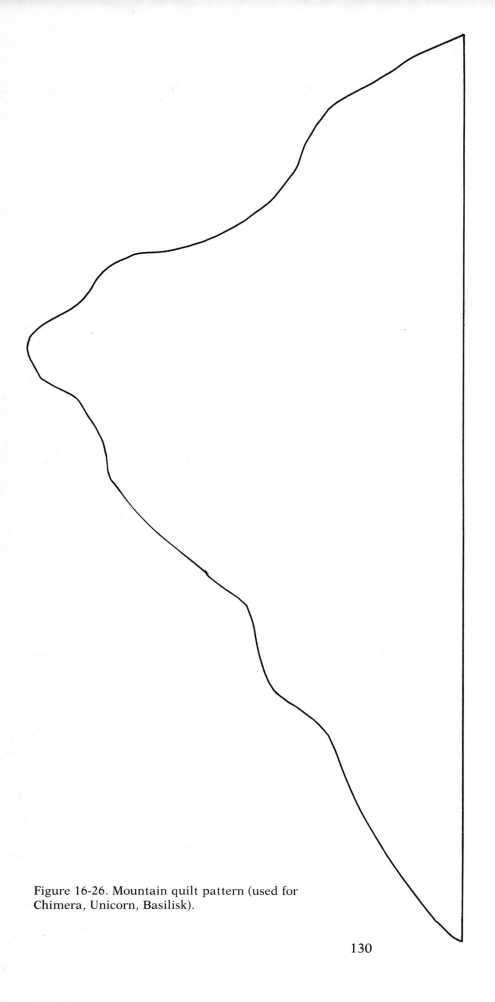

Figure 16-26. Mountain quilt pattern (used for
Chimera, Unicorn, Basilisk).

Figure 16-27. Clam shell quilt pattern (templates).

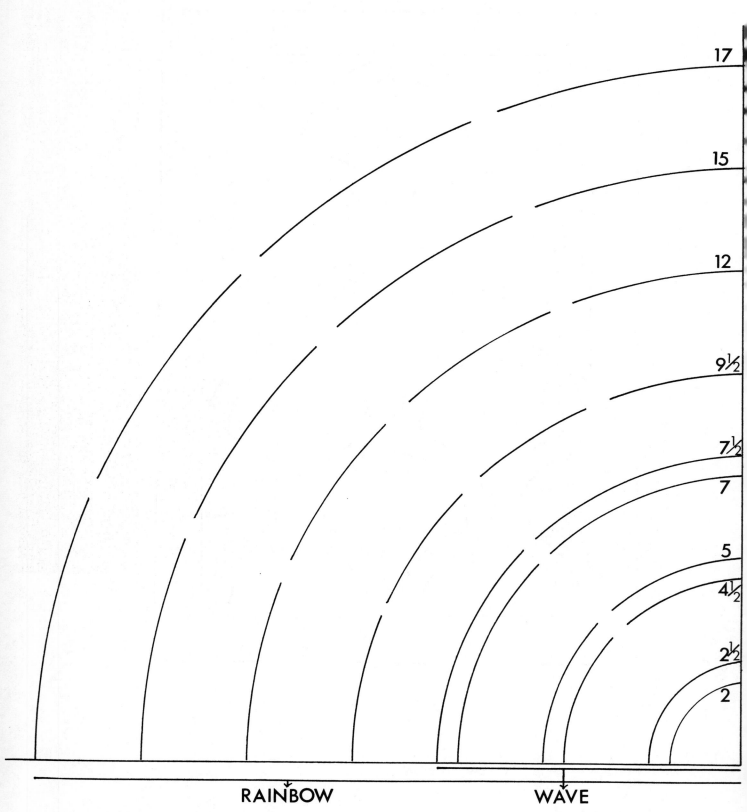

17

15

12

9½

7½

7

5

4½

2½

2

RAINBOW

WAVE

Figure 16-28. Concentric Circle quilt patterns
(templates).

132

Figure 16-29. Wave Circles quilting (5-by-22-inch strips).

Figure 16-31. Rainbow quilting (top and bottom strips).

Figure 16-30. Clamshell quilting (5-by-70-inch strips).

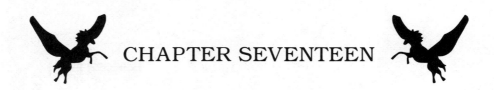

CHAPTER SEVENTEEN

Pegasus Needlepoint Clutch Purse

This design is another interpretation of the appliqué design in the *Mythical Beast Quilt*. The horse is stitched with different pattern stitches using only white and ecru Perle cotton. The background consists of a gradual gradation of colors. The purse, which you construct yourself, measures 6 by 9 inches (15 by 23cm).

MATERIALS
- #18 mono canvas, 11 by 19 inches (28 by 48cm)
- DMC Perle cotton (size 5), 1 25-meter skein each of white and ecru
- DMC embroidery floss, 8 8-meter skeins in the following colors: #819 baby pink, #951 flesh, #745 pale yellow, #369 pale pistachio green, #775 light baby blue, #211 light lavender
- Tapestry needle #22 or #24
- Fabric for purse lining, ½ yard (46cm)
- Braid trim—Perle cotton #775 light blue (see *Finishing Hints*)
- Gray marker
- Curved needle
- Purse snap

DIRECTIONS
1. Refer to Figure 17-2. The design measures 270 threads by 162 threads.
2. Tape the edges of the canvas with masking tape.
3. With a gray marker draw a 2-inch (5cm) margin around the canvas. Draw a horizontal line at 3 inches (8cm) and at 9 inches (23cm). These horizontal lines are the folding lines of the purse (see Figure 17-3). In the margin along the edge of the canvas, starting at the upper right-hand corner, count the threads and place a mark at 16 threads, 7 threads, 7 threads, 7 threads, 7 threads, and 7 threads. Repeat this pattern around the entire edge.
4. Trace the Pegasus from the book in the center section of the needlepoint canvas with the gray marker.
5. Stitch the feathers, tail, mane, and hooves in white Perle cotton in the stitches indicated in Figure 17-2. Outline the horse's body, head, and legs, with ecru Perle cotton in tent stitch. Then with the white Perle cotton fill in horse body, legs, and head with tent stitch.
6. Using all 6 plies of embroidery floss, stitch the background with basketweave stitch. Using the marks in the margin as a guide, start with 6 plies of the pink embroidery floss and work the first 16 rows. Remove 1 ply of the pink and replace it with 1 ply of the flesh and work the next 7 rows. For the next 7 rows remove 2 plies of pink and add 2 plies of flesh. From then on, every 7 rows, remove 1 more ply of pink and replace it with 1 more ply of flesh until, in the last 7-row section, there are 5 plies of flesh and 1 ply of pink. Stitch the next 16 rows with 6 plies of flesh and repeat these thread changes with yellow until there are six strands of yellow for the next 16 row section. The color changes then go to yellow, then to green, then to blue, then to laven-

Figure 17-1. Pegasus purse—stitched by Wendy Gault
and the author.

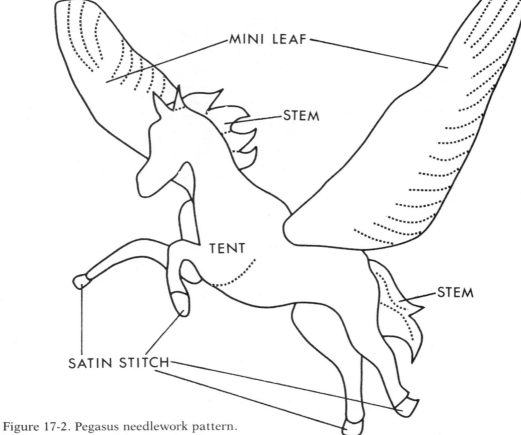

MINI LEAF

STEM

TENT

STEM

SATIN STITCH

Figure 17-2. Pegasus needlework pattern.

der, then to pink, then to flesh. End the lower left-hand corner in yellow.

7. Block the needlepoint (see *Finishing Hints*).

8. Trim the needlepoint, leaving 6 unworked canvas threads around the edge.

9. Fold the unworked canvas threads toward the back of the needlepoint and tack down with herringbone stitch (see *Finishing Hints*) around the canvas.

10. Fold the needlepoint at the 9-inch (23cm) line. Using the ladder stitch along the outside of the purse, sew the two side edges.

11. Cut a piece of lining fabric 10 by 16 inches (25.5 by 40.5cm). Fold, with right sides together, a 6½ inch (16.5cm) pocket. Sew a ½-inch (1cm) seam along the edges of this pocket, leaving ½ inch open at the top of the seam on both sides. Fold ½ inch to the back of lining on the flap and front of the pocket. Press.

12. Insert the lining into the canvas purse, with wrong sides facing each other. Tack the lining to the needlepoint at the opening and along the flap with herringbone or whipstitch, hiding all unworked canvas threads.

13. Stitch a Perle cotton braid around all edges with a whipstitch.

14. Place a snap on the front and the flap of the purse for closing.

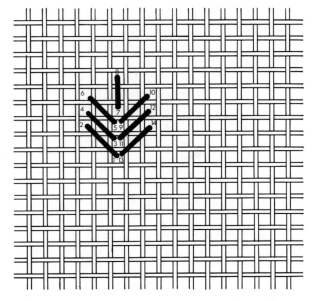

Figure 17-4. Mini leaf stitch.

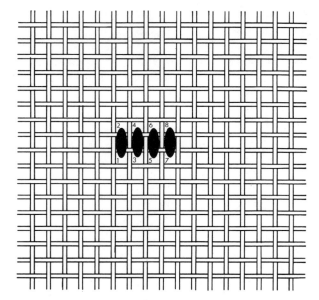

Figure 17-5. Satin stitch.

Figure 17-3. Purse measurements.

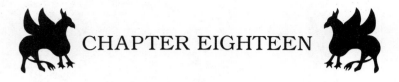

CHAPTER EIGHTEEN

Phoenix Blackwork Mounted Picture

The mythical beast creatures used in the quilt on page 110 lend themselves to blackwork because of the large open spaces in the designs. Any of the quilt designs can be traced from this book onto needlepoint canvas and stitched with blackwork patterns. This phoenix makes an attractive blackwork picture. The finished design measures 9½ by 9½ inches (24 by 24cm).

MATERIALS

- #18 mono canvas, 12 by 12 inches (30.5 by 30.5cm)
- DMC embroidery floss, 5 8-meter skeins of #3371 black
- Balger #16 gold embroidery thread, 1 10-meter skein of gold
- Tapestry needle #22
- Embroidery needle
- Gray marker
- Stretcher bars

DIRECTIONS

1. Using Figure 18-2 trace the design in the center of the canvas, using a gray marker. Lightly mark a 2-inch (5cm) margin around the edge of the canvas.
2. This design can be stitched without a frame. However, you might find it easier to mount it on the stretcher bars that many needlecraft stores carry for this purpose. These stretcher bars would be, in most cases, too long for framing the picture afterwards. Tape the edges of the canvas with masking tape and staple the canvas to the top of the stretcher bars through the masking tape.
3. Using Figures 18-2 and 18-3 as references, stitch the appropriate patterns in the pheonix design with 3 plies embroidery floss and tapestry needle. The letters in Figure 18-2 correspond to the stitch patterns in Figure 18-3.
4. With gold thread, make French knots for the eye.
5. With 3 plies of embroidery floss and the embroidery needle, outline the design.
6. Remove from stretcher bars when design is complete. Frame the design with a white piece of ragboard behind the needlepoint canvas (see *Finishing Hints*).

Figure 18-1. Blackwork
Phoenix—stitched by the
author.

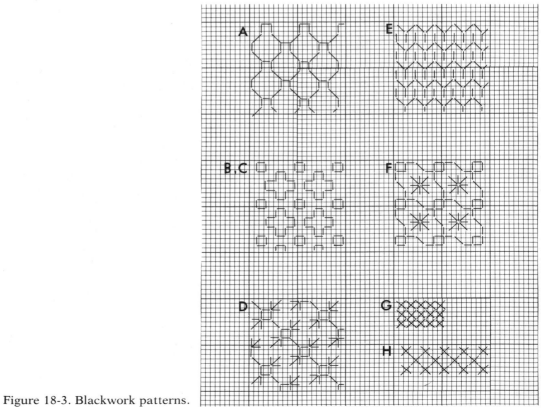

Figure 18-3. Blackwork patterns.

Figure 18-2. Blackwork pattern placement on Phoenix.

 CHAPTER NINETEEN

Green Dragon Needlepoint Pillow

For beginners in needlepoint, the mythical creatures in the quilt on page 110 make good projects. The more ambitious can do a little research and use pattern stitches in the design. I used very large canvas when I adapted the dragon for needlepoint, but you can use smaller canvas just as easily, if you prefer it. The finished needlepoint measures 8½ by 8½ inches (21.5 by 21.5cm).

MATERIALS
- #10 mono canvas, 12½ by 12½ inches (32 by 32cm)
- Paternayan Persian yarn. See Color Chart (Figure 19-2)
- Tapestry needle #18
- Gray marker
- Fabric for backing

DIRECTIONS
1. Tape the edges of the canvas with masking tape.
2. With the gray marker, trace the dragon in the center of the needlepoint canvas. Lightly mark a 2-inch (5cm) margin around the edge of the canvas.
3. Refer to Figure 19-2. Use 3 plies of the Persian yarn to stitch the design in tent stitch.
4. When stitching is completed, block the canvas and assemble into a knife-edge pillow (see *Finishing Hints*).

Figure 19-1. Green Dragon Pillow—stitched by Joann Young.

A #698
B #772
C #634
D #697

Figure 19-2. Green Needlepoint dragon chart.

Color	# of Strands	Design Part
Paternayan Persian yarn, 33-inch (84-cm) strands		
#772 sunny yellow	20	wings, eyes
#634 light spring green	20	tummy, fins
#698 Christmas green	10	tail, back, tummy, lines

Color	# of Strands	Design Part
#697 dark Christmas green	15	wings, legs, face, veins
#220 black	1	pupils, nose
#261 natural white	35	background

Bibliography

Burchette, Dorothy. *Needlework Blocking and Finishing*. New York: Scribner's, 1974.

Christensen, Jo Ippolito. *The Needlepoint Book*. Englewood Cliffs, N.J.: Spectrum, 1976.

Click, Terri L., and Porter, Pat. *Fabric Boxes*. Laguna Hills, Calif.: Glick Publishing, 1980.

Hassel, Carla J. *You Can Be a Super Quilter*. Des Moines, Ia.: Wallace Homestead, 1980.

Hurlburt, Regina. *Left-Handed Needlepoint*. New York: Van Nostrand Reinhold, 1972.

Kalish, Susan. *Oriental Rugs in Needlepoint*. New York: Van Nostrand Reinhold, 1982.

Meyers, Carole Robbins. *A Primer of Left-Handed Embroidery*. New York: Scribner's, 1974.

Reader's Digest Association, Inc. *Reader's Digest Complete Guide to Needlework*. New York: Reader's Digest Association, Inc., 1979.

Sunset Editors. *Needlepoint Techniques and Projects*. Menlo Park, Calif.: Lane Publishing, 1977.

———*Quilting, Patchwork, and Appliqué*. Menlo Park, Calif.: Lane Publishing, 1977.

Walzer, Mary. *Handbook of Needlepoint Stitches*. New York: Van Nostrand Reinhold, 1976.

Wilson, Erica. *Embroidery Book*. New York: Scribner's, 1973.

Index

Achelous and Hercules cross-stitch
  pillow, 106–109
Aida cloth, 10, 106
Alphabet, mythical character cross-
  stitch, 78–98
Alphabet coasters, 79–80
Alphabet panel, 78–79
Alphabet wall hanging, 78–79
Appliqué quilt, mythical beast,
  110–133

Back-forward stitch, 16
Back stitch, 16
Baker, Cicely Mary, 64
Basilisk, 110
Basketweave stitch, 13, 14
Batting, quilt, 10
Beast, mythical, appliqué quilt,
  110–133
Blackwork
  blocking, 19
  hints for, 16
  pictures, 75–77, 137–139
Blocking, 18–19
Book cover, rose baby cross-stitch,
  72–74
Box-edge pillows, 20–21
Boxes
  Pegasus cross-stitch fabric,
    103–105
  sea serpent cross-stitch fabric,
    100–102
Braid twists (for edges), 22
Broadcloth, cotton, 10

"C" pillow, 97–98
California poppy flower child cross-
  stitch framed picture, 69–71
Canvas, 10, 13

Cherry blossom flower child cross-
  stitch stationery and portfolio,
  64–68
Chimera, 110
Chinatown dragon needlepoint
  pillow, 24–29
Cloth
  Aida, 10, 106
  fiddler's, 10
Clutch purse, Pegasus, 134–136
Coasters, 79–80
Continental stitch, 13
Cotton broadcloth, 10
Cross-stitch
  alphabet, 78–98
  blocking, 19
  book cover, 72–74
  boxes, 100–105
  framed picture, 69–71
  hints for, 14–15
  pillow, 106–109
  stationery and portfolio, 64–68

Dragon, 110
Dragon blackwork framed picture,
  75–77
Dragon, green, needlepoint pillow,
  140–141
Dragon in the sea needlepoint wall
  hanging, 30–41
Dragon needlepoint pillow,
  Chinatown, 24–29

Edges, braid twists for, 22
Embroidery floss, 9
Embroidery hoops, 11–12
Embroidery needles, 11
Embroidery transfer pens, 11

Enchanted land needlepoint pillow,
  49, 50–52
Enlarging a design, 16

Fabrics, 10
Fiddler's cloth, 10
Finishing, 18–23
  blocking, 18–19
  with braid twists for edges, 22
  framing, 23
  hints for, 18
  mail order, 23
  and making wall hangings, 21–22
  pillows, 20–21
  stitches, 19
Floss
  embroidery, 9
  holders, 12
  silk, 9–10
Frames
  needlepoint, 12, 13
  quilting, 12
Framing, 23

Graphs, following, 15
Green dragon needlepoint pillow,
  140–141
Griffin, 110
Griffin needlepoint pillow, 42–43,
  46–48

Hardanger, 10
Heracles and Achelous cross-stitch
  pillow, 106–109
Herringbone stitch, 19
Hints, 13–17
  for blackwork, 16
  for cross-stitch, 14–15
  enlarging a design, 16

for needlepoint, 12–14, 15
for quilting, 15–16
transferring patterns, 16–17
Hippocampus, 110

Knife-edge pillow, 20

Ladder stitch, 19
Left-handed stitchers, 13, 142

Magnetic line keepers, 12
Mail order finishing, 23
Marking pens, 11
Materials, 9–12
  fabrics, 10
  miscellaneous, 11–12
  needles, 11
  threads, 9–10
Mermaid purse, 98–99
Metallic threads, 10
Mythical beast appliqué quilt,
  110–133
Mythical character cross-stitch
  alphabet projects, 78–98
  alphabet panel, 78–79
  alphabet wall hanging, 78–79
  "C" pillow, 97–98
  coasters, 79–80
  letters, 81–97
  mermaid purse, 98–99

Needle threaders, 12
Needlepoint
  canvas, 10
  clutch purse, 134–136
  frames, 12, 13
  hints for, 12–14, 15
  materials for, 9–12
  pillows, 24–29, 42–52, 60–63,
    140–141
  wall hangings, 30–41, 49–50,
    53–59
Needles, 10

Patterns, transferring, 16–17
Pegasus, 110
Pegasus cross-stitch fabric box,
  103–105

Pegasus needlepoint clutch purse,
  134–136
Perle cotton, 10
Persian yarn, 9, 12
Phoenix, 110
Phoenix blackwork mounted
  picture, 137–139
Phoenix needlepoint wall hanging,
  49–50, 53–59
Pictures
  California poppy flower child
    cross-stitch framed, 69–71
  dragon blackwork framed, 75–77
  Phoenix blackwork mounted,
    137–139
Pillows
  box-edge, 20–21
  "C," 97–98
  Chinatown dragon needlepoint,
    24–29
  enchanted land needlepoint, 49,
    50–52
  finishing, 20–21
  green dragon needlepoint,
    140–141
  griffin needlepoint, 42–43, 46–48
  Heracles and Achelous cross-
    stitch, 106–109
  knife-edge, 110
  Taiyuin needlepoint, 60–63
  unicorn needlepoint, 42–43,
    44–45, 48
Purse
  mermaid, 98–99
  Pegasus needlepoint clutch,
    134–136

Quilt, mythical beast appliqué,
  110–133
Quilt batting, 110
Quilt templates, 12
Quilting, 15–16
Quilting frames, 12
Quilting needles, 11
Quilting pencils, 11

Right-handed stitchers, 13
Rose baby cross-stitch book cover,
  72–74

Sea serpent, 110
Sea serpent cross-stitch fabric box,
  100–102
Sharps, 11
Shears, 12
Silk floss, 9–10
Stationery and portfolio, cherry
  blossom flower child cross-
  stitch, 64–68
Stitches
  back, 26
  back-forward, 16
  basketweave, 13, 14
  continental, 13
  cross-stitch, see Cross-stitch
  finishing, 19
  herringbone, 19
  ladder, 19
  tent, 13
  whipstitch, 19
Supplies, 12

Taiyuin needlepoint pillow, 60–63
Tapestry needles, 11
Tapestry yarn, 10
Tent stitch, 13
Thimbles, 12
Threads, 9–10
Tracing paper, 12
Transferring patterns, 16–17

Unicorn, 110
Unicorn needlepoint pillow, 42–43,
  44–45, 48
Upholstery needles, 11

Wall hangings, 21–22
  alphabet, 78–79
  dragon in the sea needlepoint,
    30–41
  Phoenix needlepoint, 49–50,
    53–59
Whipstitch, 19

Yarn
  Persian, 9, 12
  tapestry, 10
Yarn pallets, 12